BOSTON'S NORTH END

*Images and Recollections
of an Italian-American Neighborhood*

ANTHONY V. RICCIO

INSIDERS' GUIDE®

GUILFORD, CONNECTICUT
AN IMPRINT OF THE GLOBE PEQUOT PRESS

INSIDERS' GUIDE®

Text design: Sheryl Pirolo Kober

Library of Congress Cataloging-in-Publication Data is available.

ISBN 0-7627-3974-6

Manufactured in China
First Globe Pequot Press Edition/First Printing

This book is dedicated to the memory of my friend, Jim Amalfitano,
and to my parents, Joseph and Lena Riccio.

▲ Jim Amalfitano at his North End Service Center desk, 1981

▲ Joseph and Lena Riccio

CONTENTS

PREFACE

— *After graduate school in Florence,* when I took a job as coordinator of the North End Senior Center in Boston, I had no idea what lay ahead. I was surprised that Jim Amalfitano, the director of the North End Neighborhood Service Center, chose an "outsider"— what North Enders called anyone from outside the neighborhood—from New Haven, Connecticut, to oversee the Senior Citizen Drop-In Center. North Enders, especially the older Italians, usually shielded themselves from *stranieri,* or strangers, by adopting a veil of protective silence, part of a small village code of behavior carried from the old country known as *omerta.* Finding out *i fatti d'una persona,* someone's business, required a bond of trust. To make matters worse, I was a twenty-five-year-old working with people old enough to have been my grandparents.

When I arrived in 1978, Boston's North End had a well-established reputation as one of the most historic ethnic neighborhoods in the United States, having been home to successive waves of British, Irish, Jewish, and finally, Italian immigrants, who arrived in droves at the turn of the century. The North End reminded me of New Haven's Wooster Street section, which I used to visit as a young boy prior to its destruction in the 1950s by Mayor Richard Lee's "Model City" urban renewal project. By the early 1960s, much of New Haven's Italian neighborhood had been bulldozed to make way for a highway connector that forced small family-run businesses to close and many old-time residents to move away. But the North End I found in the late 1970s was still an intact, self-contained neighborhood of multistoried brick tenement houses with walk-up apartments, a vibrant community where people walked the streets and elders gathered on corners and in parks speaking regional dialects of Calabrese, Napoletano, Siciliano, and Abruzzese. Open-air fruit and vegetable stands, family-run bakeries named "Boschetto," "Drago," and "Parziale," meat markets, pastry shops, religious society clubhouses with figures of patron saints painted on street-level windows, and corner barbershops lined the narrow streets, reminiscent of the rural southern Italian villages the immigrants had left behind at the turn of the century.

After a few months on the job, I started to win the trust and friendship of the *anziani,* or Italian elders—many still active and alert in their seventies, eighties, and even nineties—who frequented the drop-in center. Some became staff volunteers as advocates for the needs of the many poor elderly of the neighborhood and organizers of Italian cultural programs at the center. In the course of our daily conversations, many in English and some in Italian, they began telling me fascinating stories about their experiences in Italy, their arduous journeys to America, their difficult working experiences in Boston, and their recollections of how, in earlier and simpler times, families and neighbors in the North End cared for one another. The stories had the same warmth

▲ Mariangela D'Antonio

and poignancy of the tales I had heard from my immigrant grandparents, and I listened to them with the same intensity.

The idea of preserving the neighborhood's history came to me as I listened to a woman recounting how she had to leave school at age fourteen to help support her large family, a story similar to my mother's own childhood experience in New Haven. When she articulated what it felt like to step on a scale for weekly weigh-ins under the watchful eyes of officials while wearing a lead-filled undergarment fitted by her parents so she could satisfy the labor-law weight requirements for working children in 1925, it inspired me to start my own kind of neighborhood history project

Encouraged by Jim, I began interviewing the elderly in either English or Italian. These tape-recorded sessions took place during my many visits to their old-fashioned cold-water flats where we often conversed at kitchen tables warmed from the heat of an opened oven door, sipping espresso, or talked in living rooms decorated with pictures of saints, or—during summer months—conducted our conversations amid their rooftop vegetable gardens. Some interviews were recorded during casework conversations at the Drop-In Center, during those troubling moments when old people faced eviction from their homes—the distressing underside beneath the glitter of the "New Boston" not reported by the news media. Prior to the skyrocketing values of real estate and condominium conversion in the North End, the idea of facing a sudden steep rent hike or being evicted by the landlord was unfamiliar and hardly understood in Italian-speaking households. In my daily walks around the neighborhood, I also recorded lively street conversations in local parks and on corners where the elderly gathered, in their cellars where they made wine, and at their summertime religious festivals.

While I was conducting these interviews, the project took a fortuitous turn: Many elders granted me access to prized family albums containing a wealth of rare photographs of the neighborhood and its people—old street-life snapshots, scenes of family gatherings in kitchens and around dining tables, views of North Enders working as fishermen, laborers, musicians, fruit vendors, and factory workers—a treasure trove that visually documented life experiences the storytellers so vividly recalled in their interviews. In these albums, which provided some of the photographs reproduced in this book, I also found family portraits brought over from Italy and a number of formal studio portraits.

Other black-and-white photographs in this book are from my travels throughout southern Italy in the 1970s. For an entire summer I roamed the less-traveled, isolated regions of the south with few possessions other than my two cameras, photographing daily life in ancient towns such as Pisticci, Sippiciano, Bitonto, Cefalu, and Alvignano, where living conditions and pace of life seemed to have changed little over the centuries and people spoke in native dialects with no future tense. These journeys took me to countrysides of the rural ancestral villages of my grandparents, where I found my Italian roots and photographed relatives who welcomed me into their homes with open arms.

Between 1978 and 1983 I also photographed the elderly as they carried on their Southern Italian village way of life in the North End—with their old-world sense of *quotidianita*—before it disappeared. The portraits show elderly subjects at ease with my camera lens, relaxed in the secure embrace of their familiar surroundings, whether sitting on a park bench, peering out at the street from an apartment window, or stopping on a sidewalk to pose for one of my impromptu "street" portraits. The photographs were taken during my daily walks around the neighborhood or during visits to people's homes.

By the early 1980s I found myself in a race against time. As the negative effects of the "New Boston" reverberated through the neighborhood, widening the

▲ Street scene in Scala, 1975

economic gap between haves and have-nots, old-time residents felt the loss of their way of life. Many moved from their outmoded flats to modern housing for the elderly in the North End, accelerating the conversion of their old dwellings into luxury apartments and high-priced condominiums for many young, upwardly mobile professionals reentering the city from the suburbs. Other elders facing evictions from their apartments simply left the neighborhood to live with children in other towns. In 1982 the North End Nursing Home became the new care-providing institution for elders too frail and separated from their children to remain alone, forever replacing the Italian family as the traditional care provider to aged members of the family.

Unfortunately, I could not interview all of the approximately 3,000 elderly North Enders still living in the neighborhood. Some, like Charlie Polcari, a spry, articulate ninety-one-year-old, never finished telling me his story. We ended an interview on a Monday in July, planning to continue the next day. When I returned, a nephew met me at his apartment door to say Charlie had died in his sleep that night.

▲ My relatives, Francesco and Francesca Caracciolo
baking bread in the communal oven, Alvignano, 1975

The North End has changed considerably since I left that job in the neighborhood: Professionals with few children live in converted condominium buildings that once housed many immigrant families; spacious classrooms of Catholic schools have been converted into million-dollar condominiums; national chains have replaced many of the old family-run stores; fish markets that once displayed the daily catch in storefront windows now dispense cash from ATM machines; most of the storytellers appearing in this book have passed on. As Jim Amalfitano predicted during a walk with me around the neighborhood in the early 1980s, "Soon all the people will be gone and the North End will be one big Italian restaurant."

American social history through the eyes and voices of elderly storytellers offers us a rich yet transient tapestry of life experiences. The neighborhood history I have documented here is simply an Italian-American version of a much larger immigration picture. If we look back into our family histories, many of us will find a common thread: ancestors who journeyed to this country searching for a better life, willing to work hard and to make sacrifices for the welfare of their families, paving the way for the success of future generations—our collective immigrant heritage is the foundation on which many of us stand today. But in society's rush toward the future, we have lost contact with our past. Old ethnic neighborhoods from our youth reside in our memories, but the people and families we knew and the stories they passed down to us have all but disappeared. An important yet overlooked part of our heritage, the oral tradition—how many immigrant groups transmitted life experiences, allegorical stories, wisdom tales, historical events, and family histories to the next generation through the spoken rather than written word—is seldom recorded or preserved. Once silenced by the passage of time, old familial voices become faint echoes and fade from memory.

To the North End people who shared so many of their life experiences with me for this book, I express hope that I have saved their stories and captured their images with *rispetto,* preserving and passing down an Italian-American neighborhood history accurately in their own words. One particular interview, with Mary Molinari, a lifelong North Ender and a volunteer at the drop-in center, haunted me and kept me going during the difficult times while researching and writing this book. I can still see her concerned look as we finished that interview, saying, "Anthony, I hope you'll write a book about all these stories someday so that people will never forget us."

ACKNOWLEDGMENTS

— *My deepest gratitude to the North End* people who gave me precious access to their personal stories and photographs—this book would not have been possible without the goodwill and generosity of Rose Amato, Nicolo Argiro, Tom Bardetti, Rosa Birra, Josephine Bosco, Josephine Bossio, Fred Bourne, Jimmy Brovaco, Tomasina Brovaco, Bernadine Cacciola, Santa Cacciola, Anna Caffarelli, Pasquale Capone, Vladimir Ciani, Ann Ciriello, Mary Colantonio, Frances Corolla, Frank Corolla, Theresa D'Alelio, Phil D'ellasandro, Giuseppe Di-Censo, Elvira DiMattia, Frank Favazza, Rose Giampaola, Paul Grande, Umberto Guarino, Frances Lauro, Marguerite Locchiatto, Helen Luongo, Alessandrina Manaro, Michelina Manfra, Mary Molinari, Al Mostone, Mary Nastasi, Antonio and Maria Pagliuca, Salvatore Palmerozzo, Mary Pasquale, Joseph and Lucia Petringa, Viola Pettinelli, Josie Picadacci, Cosimo Pietrangelo, Grace Pinelli, Teresa Costanzo, Charlie Polcari, Dominic Rosso, Mary Russo, Angelo Sardo, Josie Tranquillo, Antonietta Valdaro, Francesco Ventresca, and Josie Zizza.

I want to express my gratitude to senior editor Laura Strom for giving this book a new life. I wish to thank Nancy Freeborn, Melissa Evarts, and Sue Preneta for their thoughtful design and layout as well as the brilliant reproduction of the photographs. I wish to especially thank Gia Manalio, my editor, for her dedication and enthusiastic support for the quality of this book.

I am grateful to my friend, Phil Langdon, a gifted writer and editor, who recognized the merits of the book from the beginning and graciously provided his expert advice during every phase until its completion.

I wish to thank my friend Jim Patterson, who showed up at my door many times during the writing of the book with fine prints of my photographs of Italy, keeping my hopes alive when I began to lose faith.

I want to thank Thomas Schneiter of Harvard University for his enthusiastic support of this book project and to Joseph Szasfai of the Yale University Audiovisual Department for providing his technical assistance.

Many thanks to Professor Rodney Delasanta of Providence College, my friend and teacher, and to Professor Abraham Veinus, who gave me the chance to experience Italy as a Florentine Fellow of Syracuse University; to Professore Francesco Sirugo of the University of Rome and his wife, Dottoressa Giovanna Sirugo, who advised me on the nuances of many words in Italian.

For generously providing funding grants to start the project, I want to thank Bryn Evans of the Paul Revere House. I wish to thank Faith Desmond of the Waterfront Arts Council for funding my first photo exhibit of the North End.

My sincere thanks to caring friends and family members who, each in some way, supported my efforts: Tracy Amalfitano, Robert Carlo, Sharon Carlquist, Julie and Bob Dennis, Tom Fisher, Mark and Dorothy Spatuzzi, and Claudia Wielgorecki.

Cesarina Riccio, my grandmother

My grandmother was often in my thoughts during the writing of this book. Cesarina Riccio, a sixteen-year-old farmer who left her poor village of Alvignano in 1912 and lived downstairs when I was growing up, had a major influence on my life. Her old ways and traditions inspired me to study in Italy and to photograph the way of life she left behind.

Finally, with all my heart, I want to thank my parents, Joseph and Lena Riccio, sister Joanna, and nephew John for patiently enduring the endless conversations about the book at the dinner table—their unwavering faith in me has always been my source of strength; to my wife, Bunny, who always came to my rescue the many times I lost my way; and to my daughter, Annalisa, who always waited for me to play basketball with her while I followed my dream.

LIFE *in the* OLD COUNTRY

CHAPTER ONE

Life in the Old Country

— *At the turn of the twentieth century,* southern Italy was a harsh, oppressive land that offered its people little hope for improvement, especially day laborers, fishermen, and tenant farmers of the poor classes who lived in remote farming regions and small towns where social and economic conditions remained medieval in their backwardness. Many peasant families, barely able to provide themselves with life's necessities, chose to leave. From ancient villages with names like Riesi, Sciacca, and Salemi, hundreds of thousands of rural folk left for America, where they believed a better life awaited.

{

Michelina Manfra was seventy-nine at the time of this interview. She was a solidly built woman with large, powerful hands who lived alone in a cold-water flat. She told me that of all the children in her large family, her father liked to have her around the most because she could do as much farm work as any man.

}

LIFE ON A FARM NEAR AVELLINO IN 1913

Working on the farm was beautiful. When it started to be little light out, you get up and go to work and you be joyful. At 7:30, you'd hear my mother coming to give the breakfast to the chickens. "Quee, quee, quee,"—she'd call the chickens and we could hear her coming. At noon she'd come and bring us food to eat.

There were nine of us in our family and we never starved. We never was a millionaire. September, October, November, I no wear no shoes—only once a week, on Sundays. I remember my father—how much I miss him! He wasn't too tall a fellow, he had a mustache and he had blond hair, light skin, and blue eyes. He loved his family—he loved us! If you could have been in my family, you could hear him sing out, "I'm a rich man! Look at what I have! I got a beautiful daughter, I've got a beautiful family!" He was a happy man and everybody loved him. My father used to take me by horse and wagon to the market in Avellino. They would call out to him, "Hey, Misdeo!" He used to sell his wine there.

If we were there right now it would be *primavera* [Spring], it would be time to put in

◀ Umberto Guarino on a tobacco farm near Naples in 1910

the seeds—escarole, rabe, pasconi, and *grano* [wheat]. By October, it's the time we called *"la vendemmia"* [the harvest season] and we'd pick the olives off the trees to make our olive oil, then we'd pick all the grapes . . . it was a very busy season for us and also the time to pick chestnuts. All the chestnuts! Oooh boy! If I have one more dream about chestnuts tonight, I won't sleep! Too much work! In those days, it was so much work because my father didn't believe in the *ciuccio* [donkey] to carry anything—we had to carry all the heavy baskets filled with chestnuts on our heads. And after a day of carrying grapes and olives and chestnuts, you'd think it would be time for bed? Oooh no! We had to weigh everything by hand, not like today with machines. After we weighed all the grapes, we had to carry it all up a ladder and empty them into huge barrels, they hold a couple hundred quintale [1 quintal=220.46 pounds]. Then the grapes would start to boil [ferment], and the men would stir the grapes with long forks. And that was our way of doing things. When we were finally finished around midnight or 1:00 in the morning, my mother would come around with buckets of warm water to wash with. We'd change our clothes and sit and eat baccala [dried cod], hot peppers with homemade wine vinegar and drink our wine. At 4:00 the next morning we'd get up and start all over again. *(Partially translated from Neapolitan dialect)*

▲ A farmer's cave, Ravello

Angelo Sardo, sixty-five at the time of the interview, became very animated, his voice rising at certain points in his stories and at other moments into whispers, especially when he recreated the seductive voice of a camorrista, *one of the roving bandits who would terrorize the common people, knocking on the door of the local tavern and announcing his gang's arrival.*

DON'T BOTHER COMING TO SCHOOL

Life in Sicily was a disaster, *una miseria nera* [a black misery], from when I was a boy of seven in 1922. Just the thought of having any kind of freedom was an impossibility—that was a fact of life. You found yourself closed within four walls and a roof. If you were intelligent you could never reach your potential because one could never escape small village life. Of course, nowadays it's much different in Sicily. Life there at that time was like a voluntary imprisonment. And

if you never left your village, how could you gain any experience or learn any useful trade?

In those days in Sicily, schoolchildren from the age of six years spent a half day in school and a half day at work. But school was not enforced like it is today and, in fact, the teachers used to even discourage us from going. Say you missed school on one day. The teacher would say to you, "Why didn't you come to school yesterday?" And you'd make an excuse like you had to stay home that day to take care of your sick mother who needed your help. The teacher would then tell you, "The less students, the better off we are. Why do you even bother to come?" They would make fun of you, [in a sarcastic voice] "And anyway, what do you think you'll ever amount to? A lawyer? An engineer? It's better that you stay home."

◄ Angelo Sardo

▲ View of Ravello

▲ Children at a fountainplace in Bitonto

The teachers did all this purposely to discourage the common person from attending school so they could pay more attention to the few privileged sons and daughters of those who controlled the town—the pharmacist, the mayor, and a few powerbrokers who worked in town government. They were the real Mafia because it was they who controlled and exploited the people of our town.

DAILY LIFE IN A SMALL TOWN NEAR PALERMO

In those days [around 1915] there was no gas or electricity—forget about it! When it was time to eat, we'd have to go out and look for firewood; my mother did all her cooking in a small brick oven. I remember how long it would take to get the fire going and having to continually fan the fire—ppff, ppff,—you'd knock yourself out from having to blow on the fire before

you could even sit down to eat. Here you were already hungry before you started the fire and then you had to go to work.

There were no conveniences in those days like today. Large families like ours with thirteen children lived together in one or two rooms. In those days we used our wooden and iron tables and

▲ My great aunt, Maria Capraro, cooking in her kitchen, Sippiciano

footstools as our beds. Our mattresses were usually made of grass or cornstalks because they were easy to gather out in the fields. Woolen sheets were out of the question. So at night we would put these mattresses over our tables and in the morning we'd have to take everything apart, put everything away again.

Nowadays we all have refrigerators and you can buy food to last for a week. In those days you couldn't buy food for even a day. There were no bakeries where you could buy bread or a sandwich or meat like today. Like all the other boys in our village, I used to have to go out searching for wheat in the fields with a little sack over my shoulder. The farmers didn't have machines to cut their wheat; they did it all by hand using sickles. So we would always find some leftover wheat stalks that were left behind in the fields and we would gather them and bring them to our mothers. Then they would take it to the miller who would grind it into flour for them. The women would make their own bread and their own pasta and you used to bring the bread to the baker who would bake it in his oven for a few pennies.

Women were expected to get married and guarantee the husband a family. The role of the woman was to produce children—it was normal in those days to have ten, fifteen, and twenty children. The woman had to do all the cleaning, washing the clothes, and all the cooking. There was no such thing as the division of labor between the man and the woman.

▲ Pagliuca family in Italy, 1928

But despite such large families, the oldest child always looked after the next youngest all the way down the line. Each child had the responsibility to go out and find something for the family. That's how we got by. We had to eat bread and sardines, bread and olives, or bread and onions. There was no such thing as meat or anything fancy—forget it! But that bread was very good—all natural—and we were never sick. Our family was always in good health because of the kinds of fruits we ate—mandarins, lemons, oranges—were all natural and they were full of *medicina* [vitamins].

WORKING IN THE SULPHUR MINES

In our village there was no place for the men to work except in the sulphur mines. And there were few jobs elsewhere. At one time in Sicily there were over 700 of these mines. Today there are only three left in operation. I remember how people would go to work in the mines on a Monday and you wouldn't see them until Saturday. The workers would get up at four in the morning and work until dusk for literally pennies. They would come home after a day's work, downtrodden like mice. At night sometimes they would sit around and play cards for a few pennies, cook some beans and eat together—that was their idea of entertainment. There was no television. Even such thing as a radio was unheard of. They wouldn't even go to see a movie because the audio in films hadn't been invented yet and they couldn't read the dialogue. So why waste precious *lira* on a movie one couldn't comprehend?

◄ The wedding procession, Sippiciano

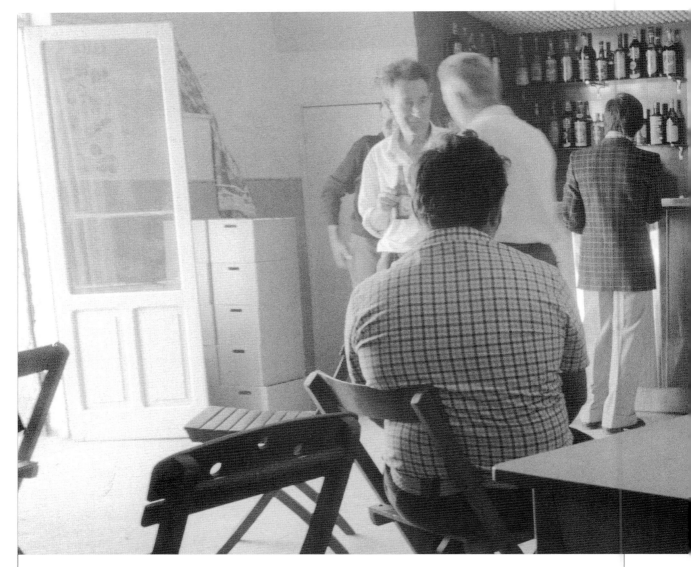

▲ Bar scene in Alvignano

I began working in the mines with my brother when I was seven. The younger boys like myself carried by hand all the *panotti*, which they called it because the piece of pure sulphur was about the size of a loaf of bread. The older boys like my brother had to carry the bigger pieces of inpure sulphur mixed with other materials on their backs and they used to put them into the furnaces whereby heating them at high temperatures would cause the sulphur to separate from the impurities. Unusable materials were thrown away and we would make pieces of sulphur that weighed 100 kilos each for export to other countries.

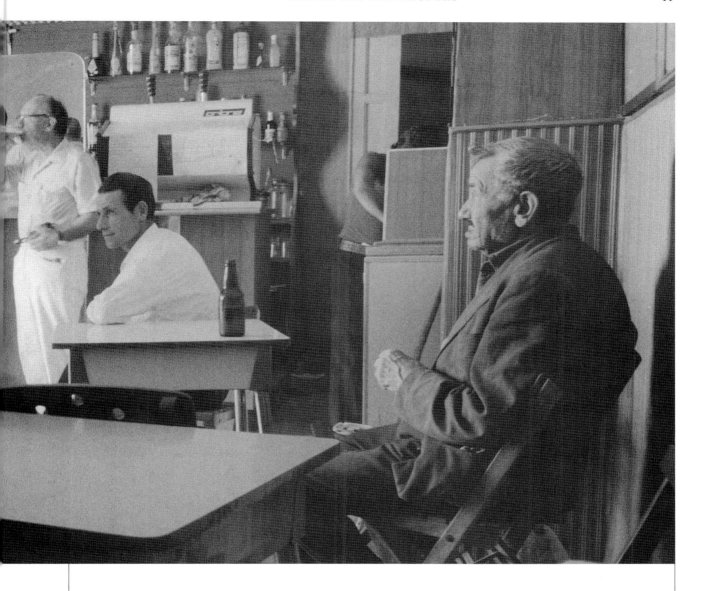

THE DAY THEY SHOT CAPOMASTRO MACRI

It was a common practice in those days for the *capomastri* [the foremen] to take advantage of those men with large families with four, five, fifteen, and even twenty children who were desperate for work in the mines. Most of the men had little education and those poor devils were at the mercy of the men who controlled the mines. These foremen would question you, where you came from, how many you had in your family. Even worse was when a foreman had eyes for your wife or one of your daughters. He would approach the wife and promise her that her husband would have a job in the mines. I especially remember this one very powerful foreman,

Capomastro Macri, from the days I worked in the mines when I was seven. This capomastro promised a man a job in the mines. He told the man's wife that her husband would have the job but that she would have to grant him a few "favors." So he tried to convince her that on his first day of work while her husband was away he would come by for a little "visit." The woman told him, "I love my husband and I love my family very much and, you know, nothing like this has ever happened like this in our family and I don't like it." The capo answered, "Well, look, if you want your husband to have a job, you'll have to satisfy me too." The wife answered, "All right, I'll think it over." And he left.

On the first day her husband was to go to work, as he was about to leave, she abruptly stopped him at the door. She said, "I'd rather keep our honor and die of hunger rather than do what the capomastro told me to do." And she told her husband the story. After the husband listened carefully to the whole story, he thanked her for telling him and said calmly, "You did the right thing to tell me all this; now I know what has to be done." And he went straight to the mine as if going to work. As the capomastro was about to enter the mine, the husband emptied his pistol into the capo's back. When my brother and I got to work that morning, we found him lying on the ground. We thought he was drunk and I gave him a kick into his backside. But he was dead—O my God! By the time we got home that night, the talk of the town was the murder of Capomastro Macri. And all the *comari* [women] in the village were talking amongst themselves, saying that he had done the same terrible things to them and their families and how happy they were he had finally met his fate.
(translated from Italian)

Josephine Tranquillo was ten years old when she made the eighteen-day journey by boat to America. She accompanied her mother, whose sight was failing, and helped her thread needles so she could continue to sew and embroider clothes during the voyage. At the time of the interview, Josie was seventy-five.

DAILY LIFE IN SALEMI, SICILY, IN 1910

We had an upstairs and a downstairs in our house. Downstairs my father used to have barrels of wine, barrels of olives. The dining room and the bedrooms were upstairs. You see, my father had a lot of land and he grew grapes, plum trees, and orange trees. Right outside our house, we had tomatoes growing—it was beautiful. We had a barn with a big orange tree next to it, and my brothers and sisters used to send me out there to pick them oranges.

You know, when we used to have rain showers in Sicily, on the roads, in the middle of the road, we'd find snails—so we'd get a basket and and go and fill them up. It was wonderful. Sicily

▲ Josephine Tranquillo, 1980

was a beautiful place. Sometimes I used to get a little basket, take a little knife with me, and go out to the grape vines, and I used to sit right under where the grapes—all nice and yellow—those were the really good ones, and I'd sit and eat them. Then I'd fill up the basket and bring them to my mother. When it got cold after we picked all the grapes, my mother used to get all the grapes and tie them over our beds. I used to climb up on a chair and pick the grapes. And the figs! My mother used to cut them in half and dry them in the sun and they got like white sugar. Then she'd put them away for the winter.

I used to go down with my mother to wash her clothes in the river; we used to call it the *scivolalungo* [the long, sliding river]. I used to take my doll clothes along, wash them and lay them out in the sun next to hers. And then I would embroider them. After I came to America in 1914 and got married, I used to cut my own children's clothes and embroider them. I used to go to the factory and take the work home. I used to live on Prince Street and I used to get up at 5:00, and as the sun would rise, it would come right into my bedroom, so as the sun would rise, I'd work on the bed, embroidering at 5:00 in the morning. Who would do that today? It was a hard life, but it was a good life.

Pasquale Capone, eighty-one at the time of this interview, was a robust, upbeat man with a rich baritone voice.

LIFE AS A YOUNG TENANT FARMER IN 1913

I came from Italy [in 1914] because I wanted to make a better life. There was no money . . . [whistles] . . . in Italy. We eat bread, that's all, just-a bread. Somatime that wasn't even enough. So I tell my father, you know, I wasn't old enough to leave on my own—my father had a sign to send me here. Eh my father no wanna send me. I say-a to him, "Papa, I wanna go, I wanna

▲ Pasquale Capone and family, Pasquale standing behind his father

try." I said, "I'm gonna go over there, I make a little money, and then I come-a back in Italy and I buy a little farm."

And that way, I work for myself, because in those days we worked on a farm that belong to someone else. We made a poor living. We eat just-a bread, that's all, macaroni maybe once a week, meat maybe a coupla time a year . . . there wasn't any money to buy those things. So I wanna go, I said to my father. Let me try. So I came over here [with the intention] of a stay two or three years and then return to Montefalcione, near Avellino. If I can just make a few thousand dollars, I'll come back to Italy, buy a little farm, and work for myself. I had to work for the big boss on his land, and what I used to make I had to give him half. Sometimes the half that belonged to me wasn't enough. And it was poor living. So I told my father I wanna go. So he finally signed for me and he sent me here. But after two or three years, I no wanna go back [to Italy] no more. I didn't go back till forty-nine years later.

{ *Tom Bardetti, in poor health at the time of our interview, came alive when he described his father. He became animated and his eyes sparkled when he talked about his father's self-reliance and goodwill to others.* }

THEY HAD TO LEAVE ITALY

My father came here in 1905 because he couldn't make a living in Italy. Necessity brought him here—in Italy nobody could make it. In those days if you stayed in Italy, you wasn't going nowhere. If you wanted to get anywhere, wanted to do anything, you'd have to get out of Italy, you'd have to go to either England or Germany or Australia or some other country where you'd have the chance to advance. If you stayed in Italy, you couldn't advance yourself because

▲ Costanzo family passport, 1921—the reverse side of the passport lists Angelo Costanzo as a *pescatore* [fisherman]

there was no chance there. If you didn't own your own farm to work your own crops, you couldn't live. If you owned your own farm, you could take care of your family and sell some crops. My father inherited a pair of oxen from his family, and if you had oxen in those days [it meant] you were doing pretty good. A lot of people didn't even have the money to buy oxen or the money to feed them and keep them.

A lot of the immigrants had the handicap of not being able to speak the language. So although they were healthy and strong, they used to give them pick and shovel jobs digging— you didn't have to know how to speak the language to do that. And as a laborer my father didn't know how to speak the language, and you're in a foreign country, and you don't know how to speak the language, what can you do? You can't do nothing but labor, see? When my father first came here, they had a boarder [system], like if there was a family that had an extra room, they'd take in a boarder. He paid so much a month and they'd make eating and laundry arrangements and it was included in the month's rent, which was $10 a month. You didn't have to eat in a restaurant, and being Italian living with Italians, you could eat what they ate and the food would agree with you. And it worked out all right. My father carried bricks, you put them in the harness and you lift them by putting them on your back, climb ladders with them on your back—you bring the bricks to the bricklayers up to the first floor, second floor, third floor, and that's the way he done it. He made cement—he could sand the cement with a pail of water—you put it in a pail when you made cement—and you'd bring it up to the bricklayers that needed the cement between the bricks. He was no carpenter, he was no electrician, and he didn't get those jobs. He could speak only a little English and didn't go to school. He used to read the Italian news, and he knew what was going on in the world—he knew the different countries, he knew the different states in the United States—he knew a lot of things. But all that he came by was self-knowledge, see? He was self-educated. He had no education— what little he had was self-education and that was hard to do, yeah. My father told me that he learned how to read and write by himself, what he learned, he picked up himself. He picked it up as he went along. He learned by doing. My father was a strong man. He had courage, he didn't have fear. He didn't have that crazy kind of courage to hurt people. He had respect for people. My father had a saw, he had a plane, and he used to fix things. He used to go out of his way to help people that needed whatever he could do.

Maria Pagliuca was a vivacious person of boundless energy who worked two full-time jobs for nine years. She cooked authentic southern Italian dishes at the drop-in center, much to the pleasure of her elderly friends, who were beginning to miss their traditional meals. Her big, warm smile made everyone feel at home. When she died in 1990, the community elders hung a commemorative plaque of her over the kitchen door.

SHARING THE SHOES

◄ Maria Pagliuca's parents

In Italy I had seven brothers and seven sisters in my family. Each two sisters had to share one pair of shoes, so when Sunday came around, I had to wait for my sister to come back from Mass so I could put her shoes on. Then it was my turn to put on the shoes and go to the next Mass

▲ Maria Pagliuca, 1933

at church. When I got back home, I'd take off the shoes, clean them, put them away—I couldn't wear them during the week because I worked on the farm. Lots of times, though, my sister would see her friends after Mass and start talking and she'd come back home too late for me to make it for church on time. I'd start to get upset and cry, and my mother would ask why. When I told her what happened, she told me not to worry because, she said, "The priest isn't feeding you anything, so don't worry. And you're crying because you lost a piece of bread? Go next Sunday and don't worry about it."

JOURNEY *to* AMERICA

CHAPTER TWO

Journey to America

— *Italian immigrants making the long* trip to America faced unbearable living conditions in the steerage class of the ships. Teenaged children who journeyed alone arrived at Ellis Island in a state of bewilderment, unaccustomed to American ways and unfamiliar with the English language.

Francesco Ventresca, a squarely built man of eighty-two years, told me his first jobs in the quarries of Ohio were carving out huge stones without the use of jackhammers.

ARRIVING AT ELLIS ISLAND ALONE IN 1915

I came to America alone in 1915 with one hundred *lire* in my pocket. It was just after the war began. The man who accompanied me during the voyage, as soon as we reached New York, looked at me and said, *"Beh, questo E L'America, ognuno per se, Dio per tutti."* [Well, this is America, everyone for himself and God for everyone.] And just like that, he left me. Being fifteen years of age at the time and not speaking the language, all I could do was cry. I was on my way to Columbus, Ohio, to find my uncle. An official-looking man who understood Italian saw what was going on and asked me if I needed help. But when he got closer to me, I became wary of him. I remembered my father warning me before I left that when I got to America to watch out for robbers and bums. So I said to him, "Are you a robber?" He said to me, "Me, a robber? What could I possibly want to steal from you? Pluck your eyes out and send you back to Italy?" Then he showed me his badge with his name on it. He showed me to a smaller boat on its way to New Jersey. But I was still scared and so I said to him, "What are you doing, sending me back to Italy?" "Don't be afraid," he told me. So I took the boat to New Jersey, then to the Erie Railroad on a train—ting-a-tong, ting-a-tong, two days to Ohio. Luckily, I met a Greek family on the train and the wife spoke Italian. So they told me how to make my way to Baltimore and then on to Columbus. Seven years later I came back to New York, to Ellis Island where I started, and I helped build the big buildings for the immigrants. *(translated from the Abruzzese dialect)*

◀ Francesco Ventresca and his family

Anna Caffarelli, seventy-two at the time of this interview, never married. She lived most of her life in the North End, moving in with her sister in Medford for a few years. Much to her sister's dismay, she then insisted on returning to the North End, which she did, occupying an apartment by herself late in life.

MY MOTHER'S JOURNEY TO AMERICA IN 1905

My mother always used to tell us the story of when she came to America in 1905. It took eighteen days to cross and she was alone with my brother Joe at the time. The conditions onboard were so bad that she made the entire voyage without eating once. Because the smells on the

boat were so bad, she couldn't keep anything down. People used to ask her who took care of little Joey [my brother] since she was so deathly sick. She said everyone onboard took their turn taking care of him. So when my father came to pick her up in South Boston, he thought she was going to die—he didn't even recognize her at first because she lost so much weight. She couldn't even walk when she landed, and she swore she'd never go back [to Italy]. Years later when I told her I was going on a cruise ship for a vacation, she yelled, "Oh no, Anna, please don't go onboard that ship, you're gonna get sick."

◄ Immigrants arriving at Ellis Island, 1900

Southern Italian women ▶

BECOMING *an* AMERICAN CITIZEN

Americanization Mass Meeting, Feb.
Michael Angelo School Ce

▲ Americanization Mass Meeting at the Michelangelo School Center, Blackstone School, February 1921

CHAPTER THREE

Becoming an American Citizen

— *Once in America, the Italians* were eager to begin their new lives in the New World. They quickly assimilated by becoming American citizens, which for them was a symbolic act of achievement. A local barber and a retired forewoman recall the drama and excitement of the immigration hearings in which their parents became U.S. citizens.

{ *Born in Trevico, near Avellino, Mary Pasquale was seventy-nine at the time of our interview. She lived alone in a cold-water flat and refused a subsidized, modern apartment in the North End, saying she liked how her old floors squeaked when she walked on them. "Besides," she said, "those homes for the elderly remind me of an infirmary."* }

BECOMING AN AMERICAN CITIZEN IN 1921

▲ Mary Pasquale, age eighteen, 1929

I remember when my mother became a citizen. Even though my father failed the exam twice—he wasn't really interested in becoming a citizen even though he could read and write English. In those days you had to brush the hand of the fella assigned to be your witness, but my father didn't want to lose a day's pay, so he didn't pass. My mother took a class at the North End Union. After she learned her name, she used to practice printing it. Then she learned a few of the questions they asked for becoming a citizen. The only other thing she knew was the one dollar bill, the two, and the five.

So finally she was ready to go up with my father and a few others from the neighborhood to become a citizen. It was my mother's turn to go up and be questioned by the immigration officials. So the judge asked my mother, "How long have you been in America?" "Oh, a long a time," she answered him. "How many children have you?" he asked her next. "I dunno, I gotta full house," she answered. Then she thought about it a minute and said, "Wait a minute," she begged. "I got six girls and two boys." The judge then asked her, "Do you like this country?" "Oh yes," she answered. Then he said, "And do you like Mussolini?" My mother, for the first time, raised her voice to the judge and said, "Mussolini? I don't know Mussolini! He's over there, I'm over here—I'm not interested in Mussolini. I gotta family here!" And she became a citizen. When it came time for my father's turn, they said, "You deserve a citizenship too," and when they came home with an American flag that day, they were so tickled, so tickled.

Paul Grande and his younger brother Dominic ran an old-fashioned barbershop owned by their father since 1921, with its original barber chairs and fixtures intact at its corner location at Prince and North Streets. Sitting in one of their barber chairs, one could enjoy an unobstructed view of the historic North Square. They reminisced about the great events that took place on the square from the 1920s when "Honey Fitz," JFK's grandfather and the mayor of Boston, gave fiery speeches to large crowds. At the time of the interview, Paul and Dominic had been cutting hair for the locals for fifty-three years.

THIS COUNTRY SAVED HIS LIFE

My father came here from Sicily in 1904 because he wanted a better living. Living conditions in Sicily weren't very good, so he came here without any relatives here—no brothers, or cousins, or sisters. Most of them [the first immigrants] had nobody here—no relatives at all. They had to start from scratch. The later immigrants had uncles, brothers, aunts, cousins—they had a job set up for them, an apartment. My father had to buy secondhand plates, silverware, a secondhand bed, everything secondhand. My father came alone and sent for my mother a year later. He loved this country. My father always said this country saved his life because as soon as he got off the boat [after three weeks], he had an appendicitis attack. They took my father up to City Hospital and they took care of him—he was home in two weeks. He said that if he had stayed in Sicily, he would've died because they didn't know what an appendix was in Sicily at the time. He got here just in time.

So when my father became a citizen, it was funny. Italian he could read and write, but he couldn't read or write English, so he couldn't answer any of the questions the judge asked him. He didn't know who the mayor was, or the governor, none of that. But he got across to the judge why he loved this country so much. So the judge scratched his head and said, "You're so enthused about being a citizen." And he got his citizenship papers and never went back to Sicily.

▲ Paul Grande (center), his father (left), and brother Dominic (right) in front of their barbershop on North Square—corner of Prince and North Streets, 1927

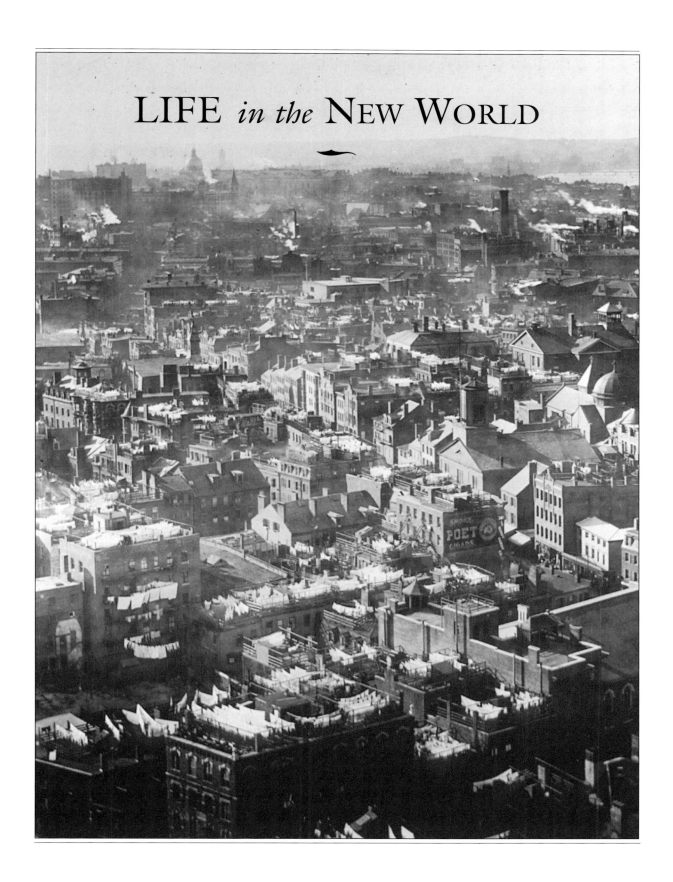

LIFE *in the* NEW WORLD

CHAPTER FOUR

Life in the New World

— *Italian immigrants moved their families* into the North End, where they lived in cramped, cold-water tenement buildings originally built to house the great waves of Irish immigrants who had preceded them. Living conditions were terribly cramped; one writer observed that the number of people per square mile in the North End surpassed that of Calcutta. Although the Italians did not design the apartment buildings or the narrow streets of their urban ghetto, they brought to them the small-village characteristics they had left behind: thriving street life, informal gathering places on corners and parks, open-air markets, and friends and neighbors living adjacent, with opened doors to anyone who came to visit.

When I asked Vladimir Ciani, eighty-seven, for an oral history interview, he showed up with a beautifully handwritten statement. He spoke into the tape recorder like an old sage, rolling his Rs and raising his voice at important points, as if addressing a large assembly.

IMPRESSIONS OF THE NORTH END IN 1907

When I came to Boston in 1907, in those days, you could really call the North End a small city within a big city. Strutting through its streets was a pleasure, never fearing to be molested or bothered by anyone.

In fact, Italian you could say was the official language—English was hardly used or understood. In those days trolley cars were the only means of locomotion, coming and descending from Scollay Square, now known as Government Center. Buses and automobiles in those days were rarities. For $35 or less a month, you could have a six-room apartment in the best buildings of those days. The best meat—pure

▲ Portrait of Vladimir Ciani

◄ Prince Street, 1900

Westerly from Top of Lincoln Wharf Power Station Chimney   Nov. 26 1900

▲ Overview of the North End in 1900

Chicago steer—35 cents a pound. Beans, three pounds for 10 cents, all kinds of macaroni at 5 cents a pound, imported olive oil, $1.50 per gallon. It was a great life in a way. But we must also consider that weekly wages were pretty meager. A dollar a day was the average wage. A skilled artisan could command a trifle more. I also remember that our countrymen used to come from Italy, work during the spring and summer months, and then go back to the Old Country, to their families, for the winter months. When the need for cheap manual labor would slacken here, they could commute quite easily because I distinctly remember that sometimes wars of competition between transatlantic lines would reduce passage rates to $9.00 per one-way trip. Can you imagine, $9.00 from Boston to Naples!

Viola Petinelli, seventy-five, was living alone at the time of this interview. She spoke eloquently, pausing at times to reflect. Then she would continue her thought with a smile on her face.

ALL THEY WANTED WAS A JOB

My parents came from the province of Abruzzi. They came because, as my father used to say, "There is bread and butter to be eaten here." He used to say that because they couldn't eat that way in Italy. And as a matter of fact, he refused to eat any corn bread or dark bread because he said it reminded him too much of being poor in Italy. They started with nothing—just the knapsack on their backs, their clothes. When they came here they weren't looking for a handout—all they wanted was a job and that's what they did. They went to work the next day even though they couldn't speak a word of English. But with sign language they got their jobs. But they didn't have jobs like you have now where you get up and do the same steady job. They used to go to the corner [North Square] and somebody needs a man and if you qualified, you got the job—maybe work a day or two and when that ended, you'd go back to the corner early the next morning and these men [*padroni*] would go around picking up men who wanted to work in wagons with horses. They'd say we need so many men to do such-and-such work at such a place, and whoever qualified, they'd take him to the job. And that's how they started here in the North End. There were no handouts. Those immigrants didn't want anything—they just wanted to work.

Paul Grande, in the setting of his 1920s-style barbershop, had a way of telling stories that seemed to catapult the listener back to an earlier time. Sitting in one of his ornately chromed barber chairs one day, Paul's face broke into a smile when he talked proudly about the immigrants of his father's generation.

WELFARE

If you ever mentioned welfare to those people in those days, people would cry. If you ever mentioned welfare, it was a dishonor, a disgrace. Today they come in laughing, "Hey, I'm on welfare." If you mentioned welfare, they'd get sick. They didn't want to hear that word welfare. They thought it was charity and they didn't want it.

{ *Alessandrina Manaro, a short, round-faced woman of seventy-seven, was known to sud-denly burst into Neapolitan love songs with gusto.* }

FINDING WORK TWO DAYS AFTER ARRIVAL IN 1921

My mother had fourteen children—there was little money. So I came to America in 1921. Two days after I got to America, my sister sent me right to work as a stitcher in a shirt factory, the Leopold Morse factory in the old Prince Macaroni building. My first two days I made $17. So I told my sister I wanted to send the money back to my father and mother—you know, they had a big family and they could have used some help. My sister said to me, "No no, first you gotta pay your board and then whoever marry a you gotta pay for your trip when you came over here." And she took all my money from me. Every week they took money from me for board and for the trip. I had long hair when I came from Italy and I cut it. I was afraid to go out at first—my sister wouldn't allow me to go no place. I was seventeen. I was a beautiful girl when I came from Italy, now I'm old anyway.

◄ Alessandrina Manaro with short hair at age seventeen, 1917

PUTTING ON THE SLEEVES

My brother-in-law took me to the factory. So when I put on the sleeves on the jackets, I put them on all wrong because I never did that kind of work in Italy. We had a small store in Italy. So my boss came to me and said, *"Che stai facendo?"* [What are you doing?] *Ho detto, "Sto mettendo le maniche."* [I told him I was putting on the sleeves.] And he said, *"Tu, le maniche, hai messo storto—adda i qua!"* [You put the sleeves on all crooked, they're supposed to go like this!] So I pushed him away, I said, get the hell out of here!—you know, I was afraid, I just got here from the Old Country and I didn't know much people here. So he threw his hands up in the air and said, "To hell with the Italians." And I changed the sleeves. But every morning he kept checking on me and how I was putting on the sleeves. And a little bit at a time he fell in love with me. Later, we got married.

Charlie Polcari, ninety-one years old at the time of our interview, spoke about his work-ing experiences with a sense of accomplishment, having fulfilled his dreams to make it in the New World. When I arrived the next day for our follow-up interview, his nephew told me that he had died in his sleep the night before. When we finished our interview, Charlie Polcari showed me to the back of his little store, where he invented a special bed designed for impaired elders who couldn't fold down the sheets. He had filed for a patent for his invention and was looking forward to marketing it at age ninety-one.

WE BUILT THIS COUNTRY

I landed in the North End with my father in 1904 from Montefalcione, provincia of Avellino, when I was twelve years old. I had three brothers here who were all barbers here. It was a big trade in those days. I cursed the day I came here. I didn't know anybody and I missed all my friends in the Old Country. I used to have a lot of fun in the Old Country. One of the earliest things I remember was when I went to school in North Square and this one professor telling us that every Italian male was worth $20,000 to the United States because they worked so hard at all kinds of work.

I got my first job a shoe factory. I used to get up at six in the morning to take the electric car to Revere—the Bartel Shoe factory. That's where I learned my trade. I learned how to do everything. You wouldn't believe it, there was this fella working in the factory, he was the fastest sonafabitch you ever seen in your life. So I watched him at work, I sez, Jesus, Look how fast he's working. He used to vvvff! vvvff! vvvff! I said, You wait—I didn't tell him—I said it to myself. I never told any-body. I never said anything to them any-way because they would feel offended [laughs]. There will come a day when I'm gonna knock the crap out of you—and I did. And one day he came and said to me, Sonafabitch! There was never a man who could beat me and you came over here and

◄ Charlie Polcari at age ninety-one, 1980

beat me! What the hell, I was seventeen years old and I only weighed ninety pounds. That kinda work never bothered me.

We did piecework from seven to six during the week—ten hours a day—and on Saturdays from seven to four for $6.00 a week. Buff and polish shoes on a three-sided buffing machine for 3 cents a case—not one pair, a case! Nail the heels, 3 cents a case. Stamp the shoes with a machine, 3 cents a case. There were seventy-two pair in a case so you had to handle 144 shoes before you made 3 cents! And you had three sides to each shoe! Sometimes I had to black paint the soles, two times around with a toothbrush, fast as you could. Everything—stain, blacken, polish, buff, stamp, laminate—in the finishing room, nobody could beat me. I was glad I had a job anyway. I said, what the hell, I didn't want to go to school. By 1924, one week I made $45 a week, which was pretty good money. Foremen from other factories used to call me up, come to my house, asking me to come to work for them. We [immigrants] built this country. I don't give a damn what they say— we put the hours in. We put the time in—you don't know what we went through. People today are getting the benefit of it and they don't appreciate it. And I was so tickled to get that job.

THEY COULDN'T SPEAK THE LANGUAGE

When the demand for labor jobs was at its peak, there used to be 400–500 Italian people on North Square waiting for jobs to work out in the country. There used to be contractors for all kinds of trades, and they used to take them [the immigrants] away with them for the whole summer. The immigrants used to say, "We'll stay here and wait for the election—if a Republican comes in, we'll stay here, we'll get work. But if a Democrat becomes president, we'll starve, so we'll go back to the Old Country." That's what they used to say. If a Democrat won, they wouldn't stay. This was in 1918 and even before that too. But the Irish got the jobs because they spoke English. What kind of jobs could they [Italians] get? There were a lot of smart Italians then—but you won't read this—the Irish got the jobs because they could speak English and the Italians couldn't. If you didn't know the language, what kind of job were they gonna get?

{ *Cosimo Pietrangelo was seventy-six at the time of this interview. Always dressed in a shirt and tie and courteous, he made eleven trips back and forth to Italy to support his family.* }

FINDING CONSTRUCTION WORK IN 1922

I came to Boston in September 1922. I came with a group of friends, and the first night we slept in the Webster House on Paul Revere Place. The next day we went to see the Boston

▲ Cosimo Pietrangelo, 1981

Common and the State House. Through friends, we went to North Square to look for work. The *padroni* [bosses] would come up to you and ask, "Hey you, you want to work tomorrow?" Or they'd ask, "You working?" We'd say no. "Then come with me," they'd say. And then they would take your name. There was plenty of construction work to do at the time. My first job was with the Alberton Construction Company outside Boston. I lived in a shanty hut during the week for three months at a time, and we stayed out in the woods. We'd get laid off around Christmas and we'd come home to Boston. I'd leave my wife for four months at a time, go to Italy, come back to Boston, work, and go back. I shoveled gravel, laid brick, mixed cement. I worked fifty hours a week and the pay was $29 a week, cash money, no check. The paymaster would come on the job—"Hey you, what's your number?" "All right, sign here on this little slip." And he'd give you your money. It was a pretty good system, you know. In the Old Country, we'd never get paid money like that—there wasn't too much money around then because we had to work the land on the farms and wait six or seven months to sell our crops.

Al Mostone, eighty-four at the time of our interview, was the official sexton at the historic Old North Church. A man who deeply respected his community, he brought two traditions together by instituting a special church service and ringing the Old North Church's bell during Italian religious feasts as the procession passed by with its patron saint. This gesture was also extended to funeral processions, and he convinced the minister to appear in front of the church as a way of showing respect to the deceased. "And from that day forward," Mr. Mostone said, "we became one."

GETTING STARTED

My parents came from Avellino. My father was born in 1865. He came here in 1880, one of the first to come here. Because he was an orphan, my father was lent out to a farmer; he got no monetary assistance, just food and board. When he was old enough to travel, he borrowed the money and came over here in steerage class. When he got here his big problem was the language—he

▲ Railway workers

couldn't speak English at all. He managed to get a construction job because they were building roads in Maine and the people who hired him spoke English and Italian. Then he went to North Carolina for the railroad. He learned a little English and stayed in the North End for the rest of his life. In 1902 he married my mother. She came in 1901 and they lived on North Street. She was very poor—her mother, brother, and three sisters lived in Italy—they would hire them out on the farms as "working girls." Then her father sent for them a couple at a time.

THEY USED TO BARTER

Stuff here was not very plentiful when my mother got married, but it was more than they had on the other side. Here they had more freedom—they could barter. Most of the clothing stores in the North End were Jewish owned—people who were in the majority. The English for 200 years were the majority, then the Irish, then the Jewish people. Being a business-minded people, they started opening up clothing stores down here, they had grocery stores down here, they had meat markets down here—and some of the big stores today like Gilchrists originated here on Salem Street. And, of course, where they were in business—retail business—and our

▲ North End women buying from a street vendor on Salem Street in 1900

mothers didn't have too much money to spend—they used to barter with one another for clothing or food or whatever.

The only thing they didn't barter for, if they went to the bakery—if bread was 3 cents for a certain loaf, they'd pay 3 cents. Now we had bakeries in the North End and we'd wait till it was two days old and buy a big bag. On Sundays for 12 cents we'd go down there [the bakery at Saint Leonards] with a big crock pot and buy baked beans according to the size of the family. And milk—you didn't buy quarts, you'd buy with your own pitchers. They had ice chests—they'd put a dipper into the chest, pick it out, pour it into your pitcher for 3 cents.

NEVER GIVE THEM THE FIRST PRICE

It was an old European custom [bargaining]—never give them the first price. When I was six or seven, my father would take me to Wolf's Clothing Store and the salesman would say, "Well, Christy, that suit will cost you $5.00." My father would say, "No, I'll give you three." And he'd say, "No, I'm losing money at $3.00." And my father would start walking out the door and he'd say, "Hey, don't walk out, give me $4.00." "No, I'll give ya three fifty"—and they'd settle for three seventy-five.

LIVING CONDITIONS IN 1919

We were fifteen kids in a cold-water flat with three rooms. Since I was the oldest in the family, I had to leave school and I couldn't advance my studies during the daytime. I used to study at night by kerosene lamps—we had no gas, no hot water. I had to sleep in the kitchen.

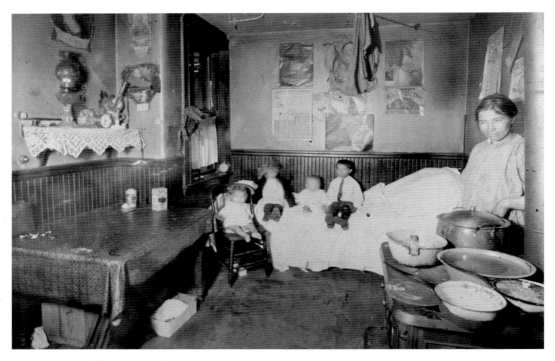

▲ Mother and children in a small North End apartment

{ *Paul Grande loved the North End and seldom ventured outside the neighborhood. He could never understand how far away his only trip to New York for his honeymoon seemed, and how his friends traveled to Florida as if it were around the corner.* }

THEY GAVE NO INTEREST

There used to be four banks on North Square—The Berradini, The Forte, The Stabile, and The Ferullo bank at the foot of the square. There was one bank on the corner of Prince and

▲ The Stabile bank on North Square, 1900s

North Streets, and in the window they had a sign, FIVE DOLLARS TO EUROPE with a big five. People used to say, "Gee, $5.00, but where are we gonna get $5.00?" This was 1906. They didn't have the five dollars to go back. And in the windows were stacked with gold pieces, and no one ever touched it. They left the money right in the window. Try to do that today! God, those gold pieces were like a tray of pennies and nobody touched it. And North Square was always crowded with laborers waiting to get work in Maine, New Hampshire—wherever the jobs were. Those banks gave the people no interest on their money. Their attitude was—where would you keep your money if it wasn't for us? And when they [the immigrants] would ask for a little interest, they say, "What interest? You're lucky we're holding your money for you."

THE ITALIAN WOMAN *at* WORK

CHAPTER FIVE

The Italian Woman at Work

— *Little information exists* about the early experiences of the Italian immigrant woman in the American workforce. Italian women were as determined as their male counterparts to help their families and often assumed difficult, labor-intensive jobs in clothing factories, meat packing plants, and candy factories. Although committed to their jobs and to their families, Italian women faced the additional burden of inequality and discrimination in the workplace and they received few rewards other than a meager weekly paycheck.

Generosa "Josie" Zizza, seventy-five, was the president of one of the major senior citizen organizations in the North End and an advocate on elderly issues. She often represented the North End at community meetings around the Boston area.

BUT I ONLY WEIGHED SEVENTY-SIX POUNDS

My mother had thirteen children. In those days my father didn't believe that girls should go to school, only boys. My father figured I should go to work to help the family since my oldest brother was in college. But I loved school. I was always on the honor roll. I was good with figures . . . but . . . my parents decided I had to go to work. In those days they used to say that the girls have to go to work, then they get married and they stay home and have babies. The teachers were very upset that I had to leave school. The principal met with my father and said, "What a sin to take her out of school." But they [my parents] were determined.

In those days, we worked at age fourteen and you had to go to continuation school a half day a week. But [the law stated] you had to weigh ninety pounds to work. When I applied for my work certificate and got on the scale I only weighed seventy-six pounds. And the limit was ninety pounds. So my parents kept me home a whole year and they fed me a quart of milk a day, and eggnog, to fatten me up. But at the end of the year, I still weighed seventy-six pounds! By this time my mother and father were determined that I had to go to work. So one day my father brought me down to a shoe store on Salem Street, and he bought me a pair of oxfords

◀ Neighborhood Cleanup Day, 1931—Josie Zizza is second from left

a size larger than I usually wore. My father, being a blackboot at the time, had a lot of lead discs the size of half dollars and he filled up my shoes with them. Then they put a diaper around me because I was very scrawny and very thin. And then they put lead in there. So when it came time to be weighed I tipped the scale at ninety-one pounds. But the doctor still wouldn't give his permission. So my mother said, "No, she still has to go to work, she has to help." After much debating, they gave it to me. But I had to go every week to be weighed because if I lost one pound, they were going to stop me from working. So every week my mother put in an extra little piece [of lead] just to make sure.

WORKING IN A CHOCOLATE FACTORY

I started working when I was fourteen years old. I was a floorgirl in a candy factory, Orlando Chocolate. It was my job to bring boards to women who dipped chocolates by hand—whatever they wanted. It was hard work. In those days, we got 30 cents an hour. We worked all day Saturdays too—and there was no such thing as time and a half. No such thing. We worked forty-eight hours a week. There was no such thing as a raise. You could never get a raise unless you worked for a long time. The dippers were on piecework—it depended on how many boards of chocolate they dipped—they got so much. Everything was piecework in those days. There were no unions. They worked us to death, believe me.

I'M NOT A GUINEA

Then I got a job with my sister in a paperbox factory, and I worked there on piecework for a little more money—35 cents an hour. But it was the same thing, forty-eight hours and piecework. I operated a machine that produced boxes. I had to work hard to make my dollar. Then I got married and all my husband made was $15 a week in a machine shop. Then the factory closed up and he had no benefits—no one had benefits in those days. So I left my baby with my mother—we had just gotten married and we had no money—I paid $15 a month rent. We had to buy coal, we didn't have much—we never went anywhere, we didn't have a car. Then I made $15–$16 a week, we used to combine our pay and pay our bills—but we hardly had any money left over. We never went out.

    I worked with Irish and Jews. They always felt that the Italian was beneath them, you know? I used to argue with a lot of people on account of that, and I always used to stick up for my nationality. One day I had a fight with a big Irish foreman—I wasn't afraid of him. He said, "Hey, you guinea, get on the ball!" So I said, "Hey, you dirty Irishman, you don't talk to me like that. I am not a guinea. I am an American like you are. Your parents came from Ireland, my parents came from Italy—that doesn't make us any different than you." Well, he went down and reported me to the big boss, and the big boss came up and he was nice because he could've fired me if he wanted to. So I told him the story. I said, "Look, I'm not a guinea. I'm a human being like he is. And I'm an American of Italian descent the way he's American of Irish descent." And from that time on that foreman respected me.

Josie Picadacci, although a Sicilian and married to a Sicilian, had a dialect so different from her husband's that when her in-laws spoke to her she couldn't understand them. She told me, "When they would talk to me, I said yes when I was supposed to say no and no when I was supposed to say yes." She was sixty-five at the time of our interview.

NO WOMAN IS WORTH $125 DOLLARS A WEEK

After my kids were older, I used to tell them, "I'm gonna get a job." And I'd tell my husband too. Since my husband wasn't working at the time, I said, "Why can't I help?" And they'd all laugh at me. [in a high voice] "You're going for a job? What are you gonna do?" I said, "I dunno, but I'm going for a job." One day I just happened to pick up a newspaper and I saw a job on North Washington Street as a packer—nails, hooks, and hangers. But I fooled them and when I got home I said, "I got a job!" They were all laughing, "You got a job? Doing what?" So I went to work there for three years and finally I got so good at it, I used to teach them how to do it. Then I asked for a raise. I was getting a dollar an hour. And they said, "Oh no, we can't give you a raise." So I said, well, let me go looking for another job and let me see what I can do and if I can't get another one, I can always go back this way. So I got a job as a stitcher. First you started taking threads out and then we started to stitch. We made baby clothes—baby sleepers with the zippers. Then one day the factory bought this big machine for making slippers. I got very close to the forelady as if we knew each other for years—she was very good to me. And she encouraged me to try the machine. I said, "Oh no, a big machine like that with three spools of thread"—I was scared to try it. But she convinced me to try it. And I loved it—I caught on fast. And I started to make a lot of money and at that time, $125 was a lot of money. And two of us [women] were making that kind of money for a few months. But the boss came by one day and said, "No, that's too much money for women—you can't make that kind of pay." Even though we were putting out the work, they just didn't care. Well, finally, they told us they were going to discontinue it—they would get some girls to come in on a Saturday [I wouldn't go in on Saturdays to be with my children] to do the work. They did such a terrible job that they had to stop operating the machine because of all the stuff they had to throw away. See, there was a knack to doing it—it just so happened that I caught on fast. One day the boss came by again and he said to me, "Show me how you do it, tell me what you're doing." And I told him, "I can't tell you, you'll have to watch me." So he used to watch me, but it didn't do any good because they couldn't do it.

Maria Pagliuca told me the immigrants actually believed the streets in America were paved with gold. When she described the stamina required to work labor-intensive, production jobs in the '30s and '40s, she wiped her brow, and in a booming voice exclaimed, "I sweated blood to make a dollar."

WORKING DAY AND NIGHT

▲ Maria and Antonio Pagliuca sitting on their rooftop, 1980

When I first came from Italy in 1933, there were no jobs. My first job was with the Dolly Madison Company, and I went to work for 25 cents an hour. I worked a half day on Saturday for $11 a week. I used to pack raspberry pie, mincemeat pie, apple pie, and pie fillings.

During the war we packed for the government. Even though sugar was rationed, we used to have all we needed. Five hundred pounds of meat I used to boil in a 1,000-pound kettle and grind it in a big machine—I'd put in raisins, apples, sugar—a little vinegar—pack it into ten-pound cans and send it overseas. I used to send peaches, marmalade, apricots, prunes, strawberry jam—we used to send 400–500 cases at once. First I'd put in one hundred pounds of sugar in the kettle, then ten gallons of vinegar, ten gallons of honey for every hundred pounds of meat. The machine would mix it up and the cans were cleaned by machine and filled up with a hose connected to the hopper on the kettle. Then the women would put them in cases. My boss liked me because I could weigh the grease, the raisins, the brown sugar, honey—I used to be able to stay on my feet.

WORKING AT NIGHT

While I worked my day job, I worked the night shift from six in the morning to two in the afternoon at the Boston Sausage Provision Company. There were three shifts going all the time, and there were about 700 people working. I worked in the skinless meat department. I had to take the skin off the frankfurters, cut the skin off with a little knife, put my name on the box, close the box, put my number on it, send it down the belt, the girl take-a my number and put it in a box. She'd [forelady] watch her watch— "It's nine o'clock! Stop the belt!" Then they called all the numbers out by the box numbers, "Thirteen! Fourteen! Fifteen! Number seven, you're four boxes short!"

So when you getta the pay, less money. I had to make one hundred pounds an hour. I had to make ten boxes an hour or they'd take it out of your pay. Sometimes I'd make fourteen or fifteen an hour and I'd give my extras to some of the slower women—sometimes they fell asleep during the night shift. When my foreman found out about it, he got mad at me and he told me, "Look, Maria, you work very hard—I want you to keep every box for yourself. And next week I'm giving you a 10-cent raise." At first I didn't want the raise—it didn't look good getting more money than the other ones. Then one night the superintendent came to me and said, "Maria, I'm giving you $1.75 an hour—you're worth $3.00 an hour—you do the work of four people." I was never a box short. I never fell asleep. I wanted to make money, I was young.

I ONLY SAW MY HUSBAND ONCE A WEEK

I used to get up at 5:00 in the morning, make lunch for me, my husband, and my daughter—my husband worked for Stop and Shop. I left at 6:40 for Everett—work began at 7:30 at Hoods Milk [formerly Dolly Madison] and I was a forelady on salary. So, I'd come home from

▼ Maria Pagliuca at the Hoods factory, 1938

Everett by 5:15 at night—I'd go upstairs, eat a little. My husband worked nights, so I would only see him on Sundays. For twenty years, I saw my husband once a week, on Sundays.

When he wanted to tell me something, he'd write a little note and leave it on the table. When I came home—in between jobs—I'd read his letters he would leave for me, "I did this for you today," "I paid the bill" or "I cashed the check," "I went shopping for you," "I put it in the refrigerator." Then he'd write, "If you need anything, before you leave, put it down in a note for me." So in the mornings, before I left for work, I used to write back, "Dear Tony, please do this for me," or "Tony, please buy me a loaf of bread." And he'd buy it for me. He would just be coming home at seven in the morning and I'd leave at 6:40. He'd sleep till 11:00, get up and go shopping for me, rest up, and go back to work. When I'd see him on Sunday, poor man, he'd be so glad to see me—he'd hug and kiss me.

> *Michelina Manfra, seventy-nine years old, compared America to Italy saying, "Cuando piglia la checka, se tu il padrone [when you get your check, you're the boss], but if you go to Italy without money you wouldn't even get pasta fagioli! I would like to go back to my old church—hear the Mass—the music—but I wouldn't stay a minute longer."*

◀ Michelina Manfra and her mother

LIFE AS A LOBSTER PICKER

I was a lobster picker for twenty-nine years in a factory. I pick-a the crabs, the shrimps too. But I no like to pack the fish. In the old days we used to make 10 cents a pound. If the crab was-a big, OK. But it took an hour to make a pound. I used to make $3.00, $4.00 a week. But one-a week I made $10, I was-a so happy I ran through the streets down the market shouting, Hey, I made $10! I made $10! I went right to the meat store and I bought a big leg of veal, put it on my head like in the Old Country, and I carried it all the way home like that.

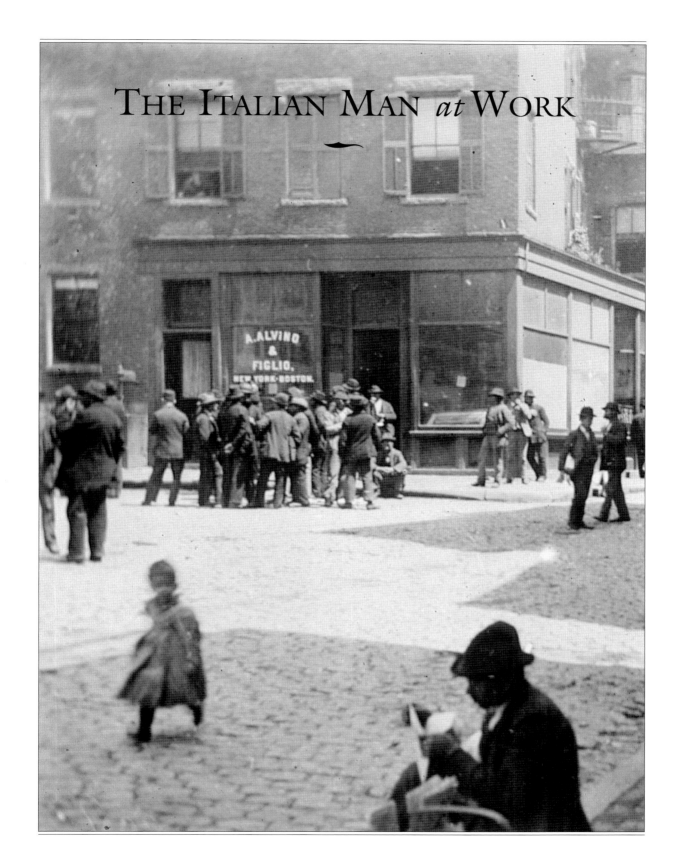

THE ITALIAN MAN *at* WORK

CHAPTER SIX

The Italian Man at Work

— *When they first arrived,* Italian immigrant men faced exploitation from their own countrymen in the padrone system. Mostly unable to speak English and with little education, they accepted low-paying jobs as common laborers who helped build Boston's highways, bridges, and public buildings. In an age of industrial expansion, many found work in the labor-hungry factories of the Boston area. Others followed the life of fishing, a tradition passed down from father to son in the Old Country and carried on in the waters around Boston.

When I began recording interviews, someone suggested I speak to Al Mostone, the sexton of the Old North Church. I found Al, a solidly built, jovial man, talking to a group of tourists about the North End.

WE DIDN'T HAVE UNEMPLOYMENT

Laborers could only work from the month of April to December, and it was their objective to save enough money for rents during the winter months. We bought our coal in the summertime and filled our bins downstairs—we'd put in a barrel of flour, a sack of beans. They all had to do that, save for the winter, because construction work, once the snow came down, all outside work stopped—it isn't like today. In those days it stopped—came to a dead stop! And we had no welfare. We couldn't apply for anything like that. We had no unemployment—so it was their objective to make sure that they saved enough to make it through the winter—every construction family did that. So say the husband died in the house—and they had four or five kids—they'd never go for welfare. And if my mother had something in the house, she'd say, "Al, take this over to Mrs. So-and-so's house and give her that." And somebody else would give something else, until she was able to go out and get something for herself. See, but she was never left alone because in the tenement houses [like the one I lived in on North Street], we'd have six, seven, and even twelve families living in one building. We were practically one family. Or if you needed assistance or if we even thought you needed assistance, it was given to you—what little we could—you got it.

◀ Mariano Penissi, ninety-three-year-old Sicilian fisherman

{ *Frank Favazza described the backbreaking job of using mussels for bait to save money. "You had to dig out the clams and shell them out, put them on hooks—it was a helluva job."* }

A FISHERMAN'S LIFE

I was born on North Street in a family of eleven children. My father was a fisherman from Palermo, from a small town called Terrasini. His father was a fisherman. It was a poor town, so poor that he'd have to steal the bread scraps from the chickens. In those days they didn't have to teach how to be a fisherman. It's in the blood. You'd see your father do it and naturally there was some pointers they had to give you, but in the windup, when I was sixteen, seventeen years old—I graduated school at fourteen—I was telling my father, "Pa, you're not supposed to do this with the hooks and the strings and the trawls and whatever—do it this way." I learned it quick in other words. Then I learned how to run a boat, a 40-footer. I learned the waters. I learned just before I gave up fishing, how to chart a course in a satisfactory way. I could go and find, say, 40 or 50 miles from Boston, going fast all the time, a little spit of bottom, probably an acre wide—that's a pin needle when you can find it in the middle of the Atlantic Ocean—I used to find it more times than not.

▼ Frank Favazza (in cabin) and son Joe (holding bucket)

▲ Commercial Wharf, 1915

OUT ON THE DEEP SEAS

The Waterfront had two places where we'd tie up our boats. One was called Packet's Pier, and there was another big wharf. And the wharf where we used to tie our boats up had at least fifty boats. There was no such thing as hours. When the weather was good, we worked all the time. When it was bad weather, that's the time we rested because if we took off time on good weather, what do we do, take off on good weather, and when bad weather comes, what do you do, take some more time off? Who's gonna pay the rent? The weather commanded everything. One thing though, my father! His name was Joseph, and he wouldn't go out on the nineteenth of March—Saint Joseph's Day.

Our day began with no set time. It depended where you had to go. If you had to go out far, you got up early. We'd hear the news down on the wharf through the *compari*. A lot of them had relatives who were fishermen. "Hey, John, hey *compari*, did you catch any fish over there?" And we'd gauge that way, where to go. But in those days, things were really tough. You had to "sound" the bottom to know how deep you were. We had to do it by hand with a lead piece of weight with a line that touched the bottom. When it touched the bottom, then you'd measure—one, two fathoms and so forth. In modern times they had depth finders—they had everything. As you were running along, you could read the depth of the boat by a machine. But in the old days, you did by hand, and on those cold winter days you had to go to the bow of the boat and throw out that lead and pull it up and your hands would go numb. But I tell you, in the 1920s we made little money but we always had plenty to eat on the table.

RUNNING A SHIP

We had a crew of six men; we used to hire them. When we used to go fishing we never gave salaries—it was the catch. Let's say the catch was worth $400. The owner would take one share for the boat to cover damages or when the boat needed to be overhauled, so many things.

And he'd take one share for himself, that's two shares, one for the boat, and the four men, one share each—we all divided equally, except of course the owner of the boat had to get an extra share because he was supporting the boat. If he lost the boat, he has no insurance and couldn't even buy a piece of bread, things were so tough in those days. But no matter, even if you was better than me, we [fishermen] figured this was the best this man could do—and every man got his share. And if you were sick, you couldn't come out or something, we still gave him a share, even though he stayed home.

▼ Fishermen selling fish on the waterfront, 1900s

With my share—if I made, say, $30 or $40 in those days for three days' work—one day to go out, one day to come back, and one day to sell the fish—encompasses three days—if we made $30 or $40, that was a big thing. And my extra share for the boat—that would help a lot, but I'd have to keep it because the boat needed so many repairs, you'd lose gear—gear cost money—the lines when they got hooked up on the bottom of the ocean—it would break. We'd sell first at the local fish stores on Atlantic Avenue, a few feet from where we docked the boat. Then they built the Boston fish pier in South Boston. We used to go over there with the buyers bidding like in the stock market: "Six cents a pound! Who's the highest bidder? This is it! Sold to Harding Fish Company!" And we'd unload the fish there. Then we'd go to the exchange and they'd give you the money or a check. Then we used to "share it up"—one for Jim, one for John, one for Tony, and one for the ship.

{ *Anna Caffarelli spoke about her Sicilian neighbors in 1980 with the same sense of empathy she had for them in the 1920s.* }

A FISHERMAN'S LIFE

All Sicilians lived in our building and everyone had three or four kids. We were the only Abruzzese family, and when the fishermen spoke in Sicilian to my mother, she couldn't understand them [the Sicilian dialect], and she'd call me aside and say to me in our Italian [Abruzzese dialect], "What do they want?" Then I'd explain to her what they were saying. For those fishermen in the wintertime, it was terrible. They couldn't make any money and the children would go hungry. The fishing boats cost them so much to keep up and they worked very hard. Sometimes they'd go out for two or three weeks at a time and they used to bring my mother all kinds of fish. She used to send me to give all the fish away.

They used to bait their hooks tied to ropes called "cateddas" and as the boat would move along, they'd throw them out to catch fish. This was before they had nets. The Sicilians had a tough life. They didn't last too long. They never had nothing in the wintertime to eat. We used to have a little Sicilian boy named Jimmy who lived in the

▲ Fishermen baiting trawl at South Boston Pier, 1903

▲ Fred Bourne, 1980

apartment next door to us. Every afternoon he used to say to my mother, "Angela, what are you making for dinner?" And every night my mother used to feed him. She loved little Jimmy so much that she wanted to adopt him but his mother wouldn't let him go. It got so that his three brothers and sisters would come and ask. Finally, my mother would send a whole pan of soup to them. My mother always used to say, *"La limosina* [doing a charitable act] is better than being a millionaire because God helps you." Years later I saw Jimmy one day in the street—he was almost fifty at the time. I said to him, "Jimmy, you look so good and healthy!" And he said, "Yeah, that's because your mother fed me so good."

Fred Bourne earned a degree in journalism from Brown University in the '20s and worked as a sports writer for The Boston Post. *When a friend paid him with a cab over a $300 bet, he began a cab business that lasted fifty-three years. During that time, Fred shuttled and befriended some of the most powerful politicians and gangsters around Boston. He was eighty-one at the time of our interview.*

THE TRIBUTE MONEY

They used to hire them [immigrant laborers] by the day, fifty or sixty guys used to line up on Unity Street every morning, and they'd pick ten or twelve of them to go to work on construction jobs. Ninety percent of laborers were pick and shovel. They worked ten-hour days, six days a week, for $12. Everybody had to pay a $2.00 "tribute" that went to the boys. There was a fella—"Tough Tony" was his name. Every week he'd come by for your $2.00—if you didn't give it to him, you got your legs broken. And one guy who lived in the apartment behind mine, a married fella, twenty-three years old, from Italy, refused to pay the tribute money. So one day they shot him on Unity Street. They killed him, which in a sense put fear into all the others.

Salvatore Palmerozzo was eighty-three at the time of our interview.

IT WAS A CROOKED BUSINESS

My first job when I came here from the Old Country in 1914 was lousy. We had to sleep in the woods [South Braintree], sleep in a shanty, and there was no work in the winter. And you had to buy all your food from the company. I earned 50 cents an hour, ten hours a day. I found work at North Square. The bosses would take the men to Maine or New Hampshire, and they'd take a percentage of their wages as their padrone [boss]—it was a crooked business. And sometimes they'd say, "Give me a dollar, I'll get you a job," and they'd take the money and never come back. It was a pretty tough business. I ran away from Italy when I was seventeen. After six or seven months in America, people were saying, "Let's go back to Italy." I said, "To hell with that."

▼ North Square, 1890

{ *Puffing on a cigarette, Tom Bardetti talked about the "boss." When he described a system without worker protections, his face grew solemn and his voice became gruff.* }

THE BOSS WAS LAW AND ORDER

And in them days, before 1930, the boss done as he seen fit. What he done was done. Right or wrong—nothing said. He was the law and order, see? If he didn't like your looks or he didn't like your ways or he didn't like the way you worked, or you didn't work enough or you fooled around or you were slow or anything, he could fire you for any of those things. If he wasn't satisfied, he'd get rid of you. Hire somebody else. And it made no difference how long you worked in there, see? Now if I was workin' for you for about two or three years—that didn't mean anything to him or to you. If the boss had a friend, he could fire me and hire him, just like that, see? You could lay me off and tell him to come in the next morning to take my job. And what could I do? Nothing. I couldn't do anything about it. If I went to the law, they'd give the boss right anyway. You're the boss. You've got the right to do anything you want. If you're not satisfied with anybody who's working for you, lay him off and hire somebody else. He had the right to do that. That's the way it was, see?

WORKING IN A SHOE FACTORY

I always did factory work in South Boston. I had no training. I didn't go to school for a trade. I didn't . . . all I got is a grammar school education, that's all. I ain't got no trade. Some things I can do, some things I can't, that's all—that's it. I worked in a cut sole factory on the soles of the shoes. Big, big bends—big slices of rawhide, the backbone and everything of the cattle—they used to skin the cattle. When they killed the bull, they'd skin 'em for his hide. Then they had a tannery in Cincinnati where the people worked—they tanned those hides in chemical stuff, they'd take all the fur off, and it leaves the leather skin. And they used to cut the leather skins into bails, rope 'em up in 100-, 200-pound bales, put it on a truck. They got a block on a machine and a press they step on and a heavy iron comes down—boom!—you put the leather on the block and then you put the die—size eight, size nine, size ten, or whatever it was—and you take one sole off, step, then another one, and another one, and another—all soles outta them leather strips. It was seasonal work like in the candy factories. They'd make Christmas candies in the summer and then around Christmas they're laid off. That's the way it was. In the shoe factories, when they got orders to make shoes, see, they'd buy the leather. And the hours were different, there was no forty-hour week, and anytime you worked over forty hours, you just got paid the straight time—there was no overtime. If you worked a Sunday, even so, you got straight time, that's all. Now it's double time on a Sunday and overtime on a weekday. But those things were added on after 1930.

{ *Joe Petringa was sixty-seven at the time of our interview. He noted that he was begin-ning to forget all his childhood stories because there weren't any older people left in his family to keep his memories of the past alive.* }

LIFE AS A TEAMSTER

▲ Portrait of Joe Petringa's father, 1920

My father came from a town called Tuttora, provincia di Ragusa. He came alone in 1912, on his own, from Sicily after he served his time in the military as a *bersaglieri* [soldier of crack corps in the Italian army]. He went to Lawrence, Massachusetts, to work in a wool mill; then he settled in the North End where he met my mother. She was born in Riesi, provincia di Cal-tanisetta in Sicily—she came here because she thought this country would be a better place to make a living. And they raised a family here in the North End, seven of us. I was born on Unity Court behind the Old North Church.

My father always worked. He never be-lieved a woman should go out for work. In those days, they had too much to do. They didn't have modern appliances. When times got tough, my mother had to make her own bread and maca-roni—so how could a woman go out to work? Every Sunday my father always did the cooking. And it was the best meal of the week. He used to make this chocolate pudding every once in a while—I still love it today!

My father owned a delivery stable. He was a teamster—horse and wagon. He had fifty to one hundred horses on Endicott and North Margin Street. He had a stable in Charlestown. He was a great trainer of horses, and he was very good at keeping horses. If they were ill, he knew just how to take care of them, and in two or three weeks' time they'd be back in very good condition. He would clean them off, feed them the right food, and he was always with them. In those days the barn was right next to the home, like a farmer would have. In the city, in the North End, there were stables all over. In those days there were two, one on North Margin Street, one on Endicott Street. My father used to rent out the horses to businesses, and those who owned their own horses would board them just like a garage. Every once in a while I used to help him shear the horses. Then he became a trucker in 1926. We started our own trucking business, Petringa's Trucking

▲ The Petringa Brothers Trucking Company, 1938

Company, in 1934. In the '30s the trucking business was in its growing stages, and it was very interesting in those days. Trucking was the best way to ship goods immediately. You could get six or seven gallons of gas for a dollar. I remember when I first started driving in 1936—if you hit 35 mph, that was considered high speed. And you could get stopped by a state trooper too.

{ *Dominic Rosso, seventy-two years old at the time of our interview, said he decided to never marry because he saw the pitfalls of being a married musician living on the road.* }

LIFE AS A DRUMMER

As a boy of ten, I took a liking to drums because I heard a few bands that I liked. And I was determined to make it. So at fourteen I got a set of drums in 1916, and the first day at it I seemed to have the beat already. I didn't know a thing about music at the time. My first job was in a Chinese restaurant in Hoboken, and they used to pay by the month in those days—$100 a month and meals. That was a lot of money—$25 a week at that time was like four or

▲ Dominic Rosso, 1979

five hundred a week. In the Chinese restaurant we had a piano player and a fiddle player—we only knew about seven or eight songs. Then I went to Greenwich Village—it was a big thing those days, society people came from all over the world. It was an attraction—they called it "Little Bohemia"—class, real class, not like it is today. All they used was a piano and drums—no electric lights, just candles on the tables.

Now while I was playing in the Village, there was a band called The Original Dixieland Jazz Band—they were the top and they were famous. And there was the number-two band called The Original Memphis Five—they had all stars in the band, real good musicians. And while I was playing in the Village, I said, Gee, I gotta get me a band like that. And eventually I finally did—I picked my men and started rehearsing. And I started playing for social clubs that ran dances. They used to advertise by putting our band on plates—after a while I got known—people used to come to my house and ask for our band. And that's how I got started.

We made a lotta money. We were getting big money when the dollar was a dollar. With a dollar, you could live all day. You could go to the theatre—10 cents, an ice cream soda, a pack of cigarettes all for a dollar. That's why I say, when the dollar was a dollar, in those days salaries were big in comparison to today—you think you're getting 200 and it's a lot of money—there's no comparison. Everything was a penny a pound. But New York was a great place—all kinds of clubs and places to play. I used to even make records for Woolworth's in the 1930s—they used to sell for 15 cents.

In the middle 1930s I came here with Milton Douglas and he had a famous comedian, Sidney Walker—we formed a vaudeville circuit. I liked Boston—it wasn't spread out like New York. We had a band, fourteen girls, the boss was the MC. We did some talking parts—we'd call out and I'd talk a little during the act. Then I started doing burlesque acts at the Howard, at the Casino Burlesque House—that's the one all the Italians went to. After a while I got to know a lot of agents and a lot of musicians, and I got connected with a couple of record companies. But the trick is to pay them off and they'd give you a little push. Even in politics or in government, people used to buy jobs and that's how you got up there. And if you made a record and you didn't slip them some money, they'd make you sound terrible—they'd "pitch you down," your record would sound bad and nobody would buy them.

▲ The Florida Five in 1933, featuring Dominic Rosso on drums

THEY CALLED ME MURPHY

The last job I had was with an Irish band at the Shamrock Club in Cambridge—they had their dances in the Veterans Hall. I never did it before in my life. The minute I played the first number they were all surprised—I was the only Italian in the place. I pleased them so much that they started to call me "Murphy" [laughing]. They couldn't get over how fast I got into that Irish swing—just like that. You know why? I was in the pit. I played every style. I learned all the different swings in the different vaudeville acts. It's like a doctor that knows you—your ears, your eyes, your toes—same way with music. There's the kind that sit in and play dance music—that's all they know and they don't even have to know music for that. The real musician is the one that plays the shows, plays any style—French, Italian, German—that's a real musician. See, these fellas that don't read music and just play dance, they call them players. A musician means you read music—it comes from the word "music," musician—if you know music, then you're a musician. But if you're a player, if you don't read, you're not a musician. Yeah, that's the difference. And that's how I started, without music. I had the beat [tapping thighs] from the first day; I dunno why.

THE ITALIAN FAMILY

CHAPTER SEVEN

The Italian Family

— *Italian immigrants landing on American shores* arrived with few assets. They brought the family as their major institution, the center of all activity outside of work. It was their inner sanctum where one found refuge and strength in an era of struggle and exploitation. The Italian family unit was based on obedience, love, respect, and sacrifice for its members; parental authority went unquestioned. The bonds of loyalty forged within the family extended to friends and neighbors in the North End, a cultural imprint that kept ties between families strong and united the entire neighborhood.

In between interviews, Mary Pasquale told jokes she learned as a child, half in English and half in Italian. Although she seemed tired and lonely when we began, the interview ended on an upbeat note, with us laughing.

MY MOTHER BREASTFED THE NEIGHBOR'S CHILD

Mothers were mothers in those days. We were always around our mothers. You know, sometimes a mother would get a little discouraged and go out and sit out in front of the door. But they were always close by. I remember a time when my mother was sitting out in front on the steps, and she'd sit out there to get away from the wood fire in the kitchen in the summertime. So people would pass by and say to her, "Hello, Antoinette." And they'd talk about how many children they each had, and all that, and my mother would say I got seven [she eventually had nine]. One day, a woman came by and told my mother that she only had two children and that she was unable to nurse one of them. My mother said, "Oh, why?" She said, "Oh, I don't know, I don't have any milk in my breasts." "Oh don't worry," my mother said. "Lookit, I feed my baby at noon every day. I'll feed my child at eleven, and if you can take your child to my house around one o'clock, they'll be enough of milk for him too." This went on as long as it took for the boy to get off his breastfeeding. Those were the kind of mothers who were in the North End at the time. And she wasn't the only one that was that type—a lot of them volunteered, nursing another woman's child that gave you a hard-luck story.

◀ Foster Street gathering, 1905

{ *Al Mostone, in a soft baritone, articulated the story of his family with such feeling that he seemed to drift back in time, revisiting his old home.* }

A MOTHER'S HOME WAS HER KINGDOM

There isn't much you could say about your mother for the simple reason that she was all you. She was at home. She did all the housework, all the cooking, the cleaning, made sure your clothes were in good form. She would go to a movie once in a while—a son would take her or a daughter— but she asked for nothing. She'd go to church, had her own prayerbooks, her own rosary—they said it in the daytime. She gave up everything for what she had—her children. Her life was in three rooms, five rooms, four rooms. They would meet outside [with other mothers] and they would talk or they'd go up to each other's houses and have coffee and a slice of bread—whatever they had, a cookie, but that's the way it was in those days, see? Although it was the father's job to bring in the money to support the family—the people who got fed first were the children, the mother rarely could sit down with the father and the kids because she had to wait on them. And that was her kingdom—the home. Many a times when we'd done things that wasn't right, she would cover for us—they wouldn't tell your father at night so you'd get a wollopin' . . . they would cover for you. It's something you can't put into words—she was there. If you were in trouble in school, or whatever it was, she'd be the one to go up and listen to what they said, and then ball the daylights outta ya, but when your father came home at night—unless it was very serious—she wouldn't say a word to him. You see, and I can say my mother taught us all how to cook, we all had to wash clothes in the tub with a scrubbing board, we had to do everything—boys and girls, so that when we got married we could carry on a home without any problems. And the children respected her for that, especially after they got married and realized what it meant to be a mother in a home.

{ *Frances Corolla, sixty-eight and living alone at the time of our interview, was one of the few northern Italians left in the North End. Her parents came from Genoa and Parma.* }

I HAVE ROOM FOR THIRTEEN, I HAVE ROOM FOR ONE MORE

My mother taught us what she knew. And what she knew was the right thing because the old-timers—you can't take it away from them—when they put the law down, that was it. We were afraid of my mother more than my father. My mother was law. Law was law. By nine at night, all eleven of us were in that house! Now to handle eleven children all by herself! She didn't want help from anyone—no welfare. She did it on her own because she knew how to manage that dollar. She used to get big cartons of cookies—they were all broken, but they were good—for 50 cents.

Potatoes my mother would buy by the sacks—she couldn't buy a five-pound bag—everything by the sacks. We used to help my mother peel the potatoes. She would make what she called *la torta*—an onion and potato cake. You make your own dough, fold it, beat eggs and put it on top of it, bake it—it was very tasty and we lived on it. Plenty of polenta with different gravies, we ate plenty of macaroni, plenty of greens [for vitamins]. We were never sick, all eleven of us. My mother had a big old-fashioned dining room table, and around the holidays we'd all sit around it. My mother would put the big bowl in the middle of the table and we'd help ourselves and we'd all go for the bread—the smell alone would make you want to eat. Then the neighbors would come in. My mother used to say, "I have room for thirteen, I have room for one more."

Josie Zizza told this story around a group of her friends at the drop-in center. They all nodded their heads, recalling their own experiences growing up in large families.

THE THIRTEEN APOSTLES

My father came here from Guardia Lombardia, near Avellino, and he came here to work. At twenty-four, he started out as a laborer. He was a very independent person. In those days, there was no union. You had to bribe the Italian foreman—you had to bring things to him. And you could never answer back to a foreman in those days. One day one of the bosses of the ditchdiggers told my father to hurry up. My father answered him right back, "You're not telling me to hurry up," and he banged the shovel down and left. And with no money in those days he opened a blackboot and shoeshine shop on Hanover Street for 5 cents a shine. And that's how he survived. When my father used to come home from work, we'd all be ready at the door. My mother had thirteen children—two in one year, we were like the thirteen apostles. When my father used to come home from work, one would take off his coat, one had to go and get his slippers—sit down—one got him a glass of wine—my father never spoke—he never hit us—we knew what we had to do. It was a regimen.

When we concluded our interview, Mary and I planned to meet again. Mary died a few months later.

BEATING MY FATHER'S CURFEW

My father was pretty strict with us. You had to be in at a certain time. I remember one time he made a contraption for the door with a bell on it, and he lowered it in such a way so it would ring when somebody came in. My brothers didn't have the keys to the house, and at age twenty-two they had to be in early. My mother knew he was being a little too strict, so she'd get a broom and push up the bell so that when they'd come home late, the bell wouldn't ring. So my father used to get up, look around, see the boys were there and say, "I was here at 9:00—he wasn't home, when did he get in?" My mother would say, "Oh, he was in at 9:15," even though they didn't get in till 10:00. But mothers always covered for their kids.

{ *Al Mostone had the kind of presence that commanded respect, never raising his voice at any time during our interview.* }

BEING THE ELDEST SON

In the Italian family the first son was considered a second father. And the brothers and sisters respected you for that. About seven years ago, my sisters and my nephew were raising Cain in

▼ Valdaro family portrait, 1920s

the house, and my mother, who was elderly at the time, was getting a little disturbed. So I went into the room and said,"Hey, kids, no more." My nephew was there—my sisters stopped. It struck my nephew funny why they stopped; he couldn't believe his mother stopped. When he got home, he asked my sister why she stopped. "Uncle Al's got no right over you anymore," he said to his mother. She told him, "As long as your uncle is alive, he is my father. If he says stop, it means he has a good reason." My nephew said, "Boy, if he ever said that to me, he'd hear something from me he probably wouldn't like." My sister said, "Louie, if you ever raised your hand [to him], you'd never walk in my house again!" So this is the way we were—we were a closely knit family—and all the families were like that.

Mary Pasquale spoke wistfully about the responsibilities of being the oldest daughter in her family. As she described her hardships, she seemed proud to have always done right.

THE ROLE OF THE OLDEST DAUGHTER

Things were different when I was a young girl. I had to supervise the younger ones—bring them to the park and watch them and stay with them. When I matured to be around eighteen, nineteen, boyfriends, you know, would come around trying to ask me for a date. And the first thing I'd do was to tell my mother—we always confessed everything to our mothers, Ma, . . . Oh!, my mother would say, "You're the oldest one—you gotta go to work—you gotta bring a living for the rest of them. And lookit, Marietta, you're the first one, if you go wrong, the others will follow you." And that was impressed into my mind, that I had to be straight, on the level, which I was. I don't lie. One day in my sewing class after I finished a pattern,

Caffarelli sisters at Confirmation ▶

my teacher said, "Oh, you know Marie, your hip—one is higher than the other one." So I told my mother that night—I said, "Ma, you know what Ms. Donovan told me in class today? That one hip is higher than the other one." My mother said, "Oh sure, too bad, too bad about her, she should have had your job—because, you know, when you're always carrying your little sister around in your arms"—I used to get tired—I used to put her on my hip and carry her there. So I got that condition and I still have it today from taking care of my sisters.

THEY CAME TO SERENADE ME

I had a cousin of mine who was a good banjo player and he used to play in an orchestra. Because he knew I couldn't go anywhere—even to a social dance, I couldn't go. So one night, because we lived in the stoop, we heard music outside. My father said, "I'd like to know who the heck is playing that music in the building at this hour!" At that time by 9:00 they were under the covers—so he went to sleep and he woke up again around half past ten or eleven. He went out and sure enough it was my cousin with the banjo and two other guys—one with an accordian and one with a guitar. My father said, "What are you doing here? What are you doing?" My cousin said, "Oh uncle, I'm bringing a serenade to Mari-etta." My poor cousin was so embarrassed—my father chased them out. They just wanted me to know that there was somebody there who kinda liked me and he [the guitar player] wanted to serenade me. I liked it and so did my mother.

▲ Nicolo Argiro's (at center) family on his ninetieth birthday

{ *Josie Picadacci was in her early sixties at the time of our interview. As she spoke about the closeness of the family, her face radiated a warm smile.* }

WE USED TO WALK ARM IN ARM

We had a very loving life. I only had one brother. And he was beautiful. And when we went out, we used to walk arm in arm—you don't see that anymore. People used to tell my mother, "I saw your daughter with a boy. What's she doing walking around with a fella arm in arm?" It was my brother all the time. If I ever had a serious problem, not to burden my parents or to make them worry about me, I'd tell him. That was the family before. And it was, really, we all loved one another—there was so much love in the families. And everybody I knew was the same way. But I don't know what happened to the family. It's really a shame because it was so beautiful—it really was.

▼ Maria Comforto

{ *When Al Mostone talked about young people respecting the elderly, it underscored the sense of closeness in the old neighborhood and the grapevine that existed between families and neighbors.* }

ON RESPECT FOR NEIGHBORS

Us kids were brought up to respect the old people. I could never come into your mother's house and say, "Aaye, Mary." Oh no, I'd have to say "Donna Maria" [Lady Maria], or "Zia Maria" [Aunt Maria]. Or if I saw your mother carrying a bundle in the street and if I saw her and didn't help her, take it up the house, my father'd knock my block off. If I was in the elevated streetcar and there was a woman standing and I was sitting down—and I didn't give her my seat—I'd know about it.

▲ Antonietta Marrone

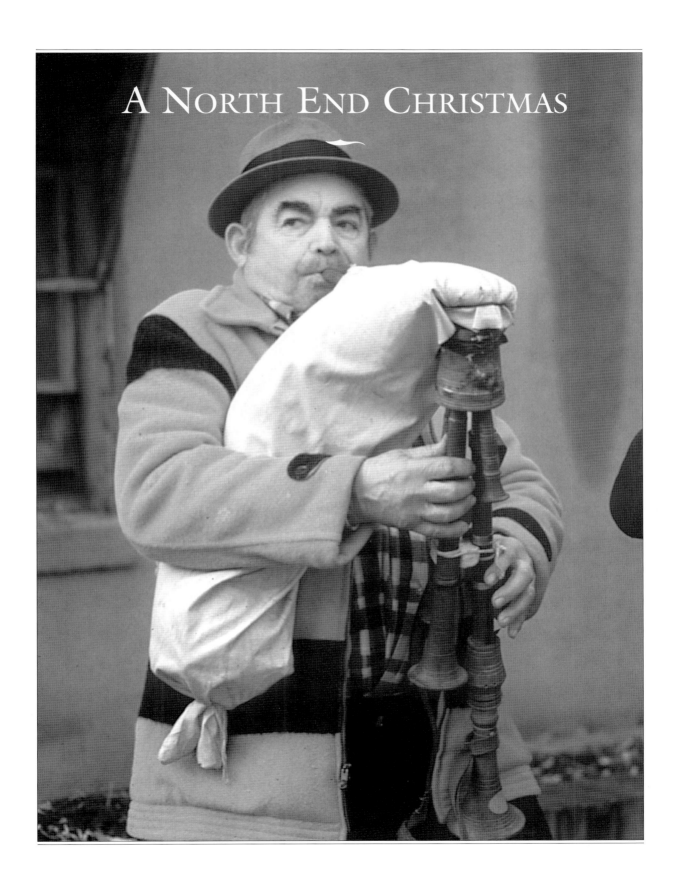

CHAPTER EIGHT

A NORTH END CHRISTMAS

A North End Christmas

"Prima di Natale, no fame, no freddo. Dopo Natale, fame e freddo."
[Before Christmas, no hunger, no cold. After Christmas, hunger and cold.]
—Old proverb

— *Italians transported their version of* Christmas celebrations, a joyous time when families and friends gathered and special holiday dishes were prepared and shared as a sign of goodwill. For North Enders, the Christmas season had more to do with the exchange of good tidings rather than with gifts.

{ *At age seventy, Mary Colantonio faced an eviction notice from her landlord after years in the same apartment. What she remembered was the old neighborhood's sense of community.* }

CHRISTMAS REMEMBERED

We were so poor in those days, we could barely afford one thing [a present]. We were poor, but Christmas wasn't as commercialized as it is today. I remember my mother making cookies and giving them to everybody in our apartment house, and they would cook something special and give it to my mother. All the different—the Sicilians, the Neapolitans, the Romans—each one had their own traditional dish at Christmas. My mother's tradition was to make a Christmas spinach pie, it was Sicilian, and she would make her own dough, put in olives and anchovies. And everyone in the building would wait for my mother to make that. And we'd wait what the other people were making—the Romans, the Neapolitans—they'd come and give us their goodies. And my mother would share her goodies with them. And that was really Christmas. We used to look forward to those days. We didn't think of presents and all those material things. And whatever little thing we would get—maybe a ragdoll—we were four sisters and we'd take turns playing with it.

◀ Christmas celebration at the North End Drop-In Center, 1980

*A community leader interested in founding a permanent senior citizen center for eld-
ers who needed a place to socialize, Mary Molinari was sixty-six at the time of our interview. After we finished taping, she encouraged me to publish all the oral histories I
collected, saying, "I hope you make something out of all this. I hope you make a book so
people won't forget."*

WE KISSED THEIR HANDS

Just at midnight we would all be around the table—all my sisters. The first one would get up
and we would kiss my father and we had the custom—we didn't kiss him on the cheek, we
kissed him on the hand—the old Italians would do it like that. And the same with my mother,
too. The other one we'd kiss on the cheek. It was something beautiful. It was a family tradition every year, and we'd do this every Christmas Eve. My father would bring out the same
bottle of whiskey—I dunno if he made it or what—but the same bottle of whiskey would come
out all the time. He'd take it out at twelve o'clock and we'd have struffoli and cream cheese
pie. We didn't want anything. It was beautiful. All we wanted was family.

*During our interview, Mary recalled her mother singing "La Novella di Natale" while
an uncle played the guitar. Mary sang it for me.*

SINGING AT CHRISTMAS

And at Christmas time they'd all get together, they'd say, "Come on, let's all go up to Peter's
house, which was my grandfather's house—three rooms, you know, just three rooms. One of my
uncles had one of those things—it looked like a little guitar—put in his mouth and go bling-a-
bling-a-bling! And another uncle of mine—*Zi Felice, buon anima!* [Uncle Felix, that good
soul!]—he used to play the harmonica so good, the type you'd put up to the side of a glass to
give it a different tone. Well you should have heard my mother singing "La Novella di Natale"—
it was part of the novena prayers for Christmas. And after that there was a glass of wine, a glass
of vermouth and le zeppole, le struffole and all these things. You know, it was togetherness.

When Al Mostone described the austerity surrounding the Christmas holidays at the turn of the century, he highlighted the value of relationships that existed between people of the neighborhood.

Christmas in 1910

Christmas didn't mean Christmas trees for us—we had nothing, and most Italians here who came from Italy at the time lived the same way we did. There was one thing that I remember. There was a bond that existed between the Italians—you were never alone—you always had friends. And I can emphasize that very strongly because as I grew older, I found the same bond existed in the North End and even today with the North End people. Anything happened, you were sure you had enough of people to come to your house, bring you food, do whatever they had to, give you whatever they could. They didn't have much, but what they had they gladly shared.

Helen Luongo was seventy-four at the time of our interview. As she described the many difficulties of her life, she would pause in mid-sentence and ask me if I wanted some ginger ale.

Decorating the Christmas Tree

My father used to make wine, and he'd keep the dried grapes and then tie them with red ribbons and tie it on the trees. We didn't have ornaments on the tree. The best fruits—apples, grapes, pears—were hanging on the Christmas tree. These were the ornaments we had. And then we had candles with clips, a clip like a clothespin and you put a candle in it. And you'd put it on the tree and light them for a while, but then you'd put them out before you went to bed. Underneath the tree you would have the crib, you'd have the Blessed Mother, the ox, the donkey, the sheep. But the infant Jesus couldn't go there until midnight. In the old days, my poor parents—God have mercy on their souls—they had nothing to give us, but what they gave us was love . . . was happiness.

◄ Helen Luongo and husband on their rooftop

THE ZAMPOGNARI

The *zampognari* [singers with pastoral wind instruments] used to come to our house starting on the eighth of December playing for eight straight days until the Feast of the Immaculate Conception. They'd sing hymns and we'd sing along with them and say the rosary together. And then during Christmas they used to go house to house. They'd sing all Italian hymns, "Scendi delle Stelle." We used to sing it together. It was something beautiful. We'd form a procession—young kids and old people—and follow them from house to house.

▲ Modern-day zampognari in the North End at Christmas, 1980

THE MOLASSES EXPLOSION

Chapter Nine

The Molasses Explosion

— *On January 15, 1919,* The Boston Evening Transcript featured the Molasses Tank Explosion story on its front page. Besides the eleven people killed, at least fifty suffered injuries from falling debris and burns from the tidal wave of two million gallons of hot molasses. The paper also noted the panic among the "foreign" population of the North End. A follow-up story on January 16, 1919, blamed the accident on the sudden rise in temperature causing the molasses to ferment, which produced gases strong enough to blow open the molasses tank with chunks of steel 200 feet long and 50 feet wide.

Three North Enders recount their witnessing one of the worst tragedies in the neighborhood's history. This event, despite having happened in the long-distant year of 1919, still brought forth a deep sense of sorrow and horror in those who experienced it.

Helen Luongo almost rose from her seat when she described her mother's horror when she heard the explosion and the fear of not knowing the whereabouts of her children.

WE THOUGHT IT WAS A FIRECRACKER

The Molasses Explosion! God have mercy on her soul! My mother was wild—we had gone down [near the site of the explosion] because there used to be the freight trains on Commercial Street at the time and we used to go down to Foster Street—the trains would come by and they'd throw coal out and ice. We'd go down there with this little kitty-cart to load up [the ice and coal]. That's where we had gone. And the thing busted! My mother thought that all of us four kids got caught in the explosion of the molasses tank. And did we hear the explosion! But you know kids—we thought it was a firecracker.

◀ The Pinelli family standing next to the Molasses Tank

▲ The Molasses Explosion aftermath, 1919

Margarete Locchiatto was seventy-one and living alone at the time of our interview.

THE GERMANS ARE HERE!

I remember in 1919 when the molasses tank blew up. Well, we were home from school at the time and my mother was pregnant with my brother, Peter. Of course, it happened just after World War I and we lived on Sheafe Street [near the explosion]. It's so clear in my mind. We had just finished dinner and the girls were cleaning up. My brother Joe, the oldest of the boys, was sitting on the windowsill. And we heard this explosion. My mother got excited. She yelled, "Oh my God, we're being bombed. The Germans are here!" She gathered us all together and tried to huddle us all around her. But my brother Joe ran—ran out to see what happened and he went up the hill [from Sheafe Street] and from the hill saw what happened. My mother was so worried. My mother thought the Germans had bombed us. From Snow Hill Street we could see everything. We remembered—my sister especially—

The Molasses Disaster, 1919 ▶

remembered how one of her schoolmates lost her little brother in the explosion. Fortunately, a lot of kids were home from school at the time on Commercial Street. But I'll never forget all the Italian people hollering, "The Germans are here, the Germans are here!"

{ *Frank Favazza introduced himself at the beginning of the interview, saying, "My name means a large, dark yellow bean in Italian."* }

THE SMELL OF MOLASSES

I remember the Molasses Explosion. I went down there. It was just like the papers said. It took years and years for that smell of molasses to go away. When I heard about it, I went down there right away and I remember seeing a big player piano floating on molasses—it was really high—feet high. Quite a few people died.

The Sacco and Vanzetti protest march ▶

SACCO *and* VANZETTI

▲ Bartolomeo Vanzetti (left) and Nicolo Sacco (right)

CHAPTER TEN

Sacco and Vanzetti

⎯ *On August 22, 1927 Nicolo Sacco and Bartolomeo Vanzetti,* two activist immigrants who openly supported worker causes, were sent to the electric chair for the murder of a paymaster and a guard of a shoe company in South Braintree, Massachusetts. During the seven-year trial where conflicting evidence and key testimonies in their defense were suppressed by Judge Thayer, their executions provoked outcries and mass demonstrations from workers around the world who saw their own fates in dramatic replica in Massachusetts.

Nearly sixty years later, the trial and execution of Sacco and Vanzetti remained a vivid memory for many elderly Italians, who remembered the trial proceedings, the protest marches on their behalf, and the funeral arrangements that no undertaker would accept. To many North Enders, Sacco and Vanzetti were innocent victims caught in an unjust American legal system in search of a culprit.

Fred Bourne re-created the drama in Charlestown in one of the most controversial executions in American history as he described the reaction of the crowd when the electrocution of Sacco and Vanzetti took place.

THE LIGHTS WENT DIM

All the young people at the time [1927] were very curious, so we went to Charlestown and stood outside the prison walls. It was crowded with people from the North End, so when they threw the switch, the lights went dim throughout the prison. When those lights went drrring, everyone let up a howl against the execution. They were standing outside the gates by the hundreds. You could see it go dim once, go dim twice, go dim . . . they probably give you four or five shots. To the end, Sacco and Vanzetti maintained their innocence, and people became vehement because they felt Italians were being picked on—like the Irish were picked on. [They felt] they were using them as an example. In the opinion of, I'd say, 95 percent of the Italian people, they were innocent. However, they did go to the chair. There were demonstrations. There were appeals. One guy, for instance, offered himself to the authorities in exchange for their freedom. No one paid any attention. They just put 'em in the chair and pulled the switch, that's all. And even today, there's still controversy whether or not they were guilty because they were actually convicted on the word of another man. They weren't identified by the people who were held up and shot. They were identified by some bum who went back to Italy. He was already in the Charlestown Street Jail and was already implicated, and to save himself he became the stool pigeon. Of course, Sacco was a very inoffensive-looking man, and I remember his picture very well. Vanzetti was a big, husky, mustacioed guy. And this other bum [the stool pigeon] looked like a weasel, which he was. Even today amongst the Italians it's still a controversial subject and it's been years since they were executed. But I do remember them dimming the lights in Charlestown at that prison.

{ *Phil D'ellasandro felt that people of the modern era "don't even have the time to bless themselves and to say thank God for the day."* }

THE SACCO AND VANZETTI PROCESSION

What stands out in my mind when Sacco and Vanzetti were electrocuted was that there was no undertaker to take them, so Langone's on Hanover Street, who were undertakers, took them. They took care of a procession for Sacco and Vanzetti that started on Hanover Street in the North End that went all the way up Tremont Street. The mounted police had to disperse the crowds—there were thousands. There were no automobiles in those days, just horse and wagon teams, but they had automobiles as funeral cars for them—I have no idea where they came from. August 1927 was one of the greatest events in the North End. Of course, Sacco and Vanzetti didn't believe in our form of goverment here, so they were electrocuted. Governor Fuller was the governor at the time. As we went up to the Boston Commons [in the procession], they dispersed the crowds, and the funeral continued to the crematorium in Forrest Hills.

THE DEPRESSION YEARS

CHAPTER ELEVEN

The Depression Years

— *The economic crisis* of the Great Depression reminded many North Enders of the terrible economic conditions they had left behind in Italy. A strong belief in neighborhood identity and helping those in need enabled North Enders to survive the hard times.

{ *Giuseppe DiCenso was seventy-nine at the time of our interview.* }

I DIDN'T SEE
MY WIFE FOR SEVEN YEARS

A lot of people here took their families back to Italy during the Depression. They couldn't support them because there was no work. At least in Italy they had a place, maybe a little land. I had land there too. But working the land, what money is there in working the land? In the small towns, farm work would be just enough to live. See, everybody worked on the farm, and on the farm you'd plant everything and have to wait six months before you'd have any crops to sell—and you'd make just enough to live. And you'd have to work from sunrise to sundown for 40 cents a day, the work wasn't steady—they'd call you only when they needed you. All we could do was eat. I liked it here because the pay was better and you could make a better living. I used to go back and forth, stay there for two or three years—come back for four years. In 1933 I went from a laborer to the engineers union—I ran heavy machinery. In 1933 we dropped from 75 cents an hour in 1929 to 35 cents an hour in 1933. And you couldn't get work. From 75 cents to 35 cents, what the hell are you gonna do with $19 a week? It was tough. Food was cheap, but you didn't get money. When you're young, you spend the money—so when you don't get it, where could you spend it? In 1939, I was in Italy when the war broke out. I didn't see my wife for seven years.

◀ Giuseppe DiCenso, 1980

At the time of our interview, Josie Picadacci was deeply concerned about her elderly neighbors who were left alone to fend for themselves. Josie, who lived alone, often baked things for them.

ANYBODY WHO HAD ANYTHING WOULD SHARE IT

I was married and my husband was a truck driver. The market crashed and I had two kids at the time. They almost shut off my gas. So the fella [from the gas company] came over to shut off my gas and was so good about it—this is how people were at the time—he says, "Lady, I'll have to shut off your gas." So I said, "Well, if you have to, then shut it. I have no money," I said. He thought about it a second and said, "You know what, I think you need it more than they do." And he didn't shut off my gas. You don't see people like that anymore. They were really beautiful people—that's all I can say.

During the Depression, people were close [in the North End] because people were in the same position and no one had more than the other one. So naturally, they were close together, if they could help one another, they would. I know one time I had a friend who couldn't even afford an ice cream for her kids, and I used to take my kids and her kids to Burden's Drug Store and buy an ice cream for her kids and my kids. Maybe I had a little more than her—I could never buy it for my kids and not for hers—and this is how it was. Anybody who had anything would share it. And it was beautiful. That was the North End at that time. Everyone knew everyone; we never were afraid and we never locked our doors.

Frank Corolla, sixty-eight at the time of our interview, ran a small shoeshine store on Hanover Street.

UNLOADING FREIGHT CARS

I used to unload semolina sacks for Prince Macaroni—they had fifty-ton freight cars that pulled right into the building. I used to work two or three hours, all alone in the car, picking up 100-pound bags, putting them on a conveyor belt that used to go upstairs. There'd be two men that used to take them off. Then sometimes they'd have bags—they used to come in 200 pounds—I used to be all alone in there—75, 100 ton in the freight car—I used to pick up the 200-pound bags, carry them the length of the freight car—30 feet, put it on a belt—the two men upstairs couldn't keep up with me. Two-hundred-pound bags, pick em up [laughs]—I'd get $3.00 to unload a fifty-ton freight car. I was working for the WPA and I used to do that work on the side—three men—two upstairs, one man in the freight cars and we'd take turns. We'd get $10 per car and split it. Sometimes we'd get two freight cars—boy, $6.00 was a lot of money!

▲ Frank Corolla in his shoeshine shop, 1981

After all the years that I worked, you'd think I should be able to take a trip, but I can't because I raised my kids. I gave them the best of everything, you know—the best that I could—shoes, whatever, it was always the best. I remember my wife—two, three in the morning—ironing their dresses for school the next morning. Now they go with dungarees. In those days, they didn't have diapers like today. We used to take them, put them on the old scrub boards, wash them by hand, take the clothes, hang them up on the roof so they could get the nice fresh air. Today we get—what do you call 'em—pampers? Put them on and throw them out the window! My poor wife—no washing machine, all on the scrub board with six kids, all by hand. The oldest was eight years old; we had twins too. We used to have to boil [sterilize] the bottles every time she used them—thirty-two bottles a day to feed them. Today everything they feed from jars. Thirty-two bottles every day! She worked so hard around those kids.

Frances Lauro was seventy-eight when she gave this interview. She often baked bread at home, leaving small round loaves on my desk.

COME BACK WHEN SCHOOL STARTS

▲ Frances Lauro, 1906

During the Depression my husband worked in a confectionary company as a candy cutter. He only made $40 a week. And with five children everything had to come out of that check. The rent was $15 a month with two rooms. After feeding five children, I had no washing machine—everything was by hand. It was really tough. I had to buy my coal for the stove for our heat. One time I went down to the welfare department—my neighbors told me to go there because I had five small children. So me, like a dummy, I went up there. And I told them. They said, "Where does your husband work?" So I told them that he worked in a confectionary factory. So they got on the telephone—honest to God—and they connected to where my husband worked and they told the person that they'd help when school started—in other words, they didn't want to give me anything. I said to them, "I'm not looking for money—at least give me some coal to heat up my house. If you don't believe me, I told them, come down and investigate the condition of my house." They didn't come down. They didn't give me any coal or any money. I went home and cried that whole afternoon. That day I said I don't want to go no place no more. I had to manage. You know what I had to do? I had a little insurance, 25 cents insurance. My landlord was very nice to me. He used to come up for the rent money and I'd say, "Gee," and he'd go right away. So I used to cash in my insurance check to pay the rent. Sometimes I owed the landlord three months' rent. The insurance wasn't much because it was only 25 cents, but it helped me pay the rent. I used to buy a big bag of flour to make our own bread—I still do it today.

▲ Antonio, Maria, and Linda Pagliuca in 1935

Maria Pagluica kept her kitchen in the senior citizen drop-in center well-stocked—with the help of a few volunteers, she could transform the center into a soup kitchen, cooking full-course meals for hundreds of neighborhood elderly.

MEMORIES OF THE DEPRESSION

My husband took me from Italy in 1933. There *la vita* [life] was terrible. When I came to the North End, I started work for 25 cents an hour and I made $9.00 week. My *paesana* [a woman from my town in Italy] took care of my daughter during the week and I'd give her $4.00 so all I made was $5.00 a week. Things were very difficult. My daughter, husband, and I lived in three rooms—no heat, no bathroom, no hot water for $8.00 a month.

I used to go down the market and buy potatoes cheap—25 cents for fifty pounds—and carry them home on my head. My husband worked pick and shovel for 35 cents an hour. Everyone was working on the WPA—go in line and get milk and the WPA give a three quart milk, some bread, some fruit to the poor people. From 1934 to 1936, no money over here, nobody work, everybody go with the welfare. Buy the macaroni, three pounds for 10 cents, the pork chops 14 cents a pound, but who had money? To buy a leg of lamb would cost me $1.50. I work all week for $1.50, and I spend it on that? No, I make macaroni and beans. Every day. Sometimes I used to cook three pounds of spaghetti at night and eat it the next few days because I had no gas. Couldn't buy coal—no money. My husband would look for lumber when the ocean would bring it in. Then we'd use it in the stove.

Michelina Manfra related how she divided her meager Social Security check every month. She made little piles of cash on her bed, one for the rent, one for her other bills, and always set aside a quarter for Nino the ubriaco, *the drunkard, who lived downstairs.*

WE MANAGED

The men—seven months no work and five months goin' to work. We earned 45 cents an hour. We managed. We never go on the city [asked for public assistance]. We never go borrow five dollars from somebody else. So we ate pasta fagioli. I made my bread and the kids eat. I buy the sack of flour and make the shirts from the sacks for my sons, the slips—all by hand.

ITALIAN SOCIETIES

▲ The Madonna del Soccorso Society, 1900

CHAPTER TWELVE

Italian Societies

— *Benevolent organizations tied to local churches,* known as confraternities in Italy, have existed since the Renaissance. In the North End, as in Italy, these organizations assumed a secular role as a grassroots social service agency assisting those in need. The "societies" played a major role in organizing religious street processions venerating the patron saints of their home villages. By the 1970s, this old Italian tradition had evolved into a commercial venture, attracting tourists and outsiders as money-making summer affairs, and their original religious meaning was lost.

Speaking like a local historian, Al Mostone explained the importance of the societies in the Italian community as an independent source of community assistance for needy families before public assistance.

THE ROLE OF THE OLD SOCIETIES IN THE NORTH END

Each town from Italy would have their own society in the North End—like the Society of Maria Santissima Incoronata. My father belonged to seven of them. They'd pay 75 cents a month to the society. They had a benefit, those societies—they'd get $7.00 a week if they were sick—they tried to build up the treasury so they could protect the members themselves. They would have what they called a *bicchierata*, a nice little party for the families together, or they'd run a dance at Saint John's Hall and they'd sell tickets and that would go into the coffers of their own society. And whenever there was a parade—like the Columbus Day parade—it used to start in the North End years ago. Every society would be out in full regalia—they'd have their badges on their chests, and their hats on their heads, and they'd march in the parade. It was quite popular in those days [the parades], and once a year they'd have a Mass said in whatever church they belonged to, whether it was Sacred Heart [Sicilian] or Saint Leonard's [Neapolitan] or Saint Stephan's or Saint Mary's—they'd have a Mass said on the day of the feast [which was the saint's day], and the Sicilians, the Calabrese, every town had their own. Once a month they used to rent a hall [one on the corner of Snow Hill and Prince Street] for their meetings.

One of their biggest things was to try to get a set of American flags and Italian flags all done in silk and embroidered in gold and silver. And they had a big time during what was "The Baptism of the Flags." They would bring these flags to the church, bless them, and baptize them—they called it *Il Battesimo delle Bandieri*. And they used to have a big time! Open the hall up to everybody . . . have all kinds of beer by the keg, peanuts, biscuits, sandwiches—you name it, they had everything.

▼ The San Panteleone Women's Society

THE FEAST of SAINT ROCCO

CHAPTER THIRTEEN

The Feast of Saint Rocco

"Quando passa il santo, la fest è finita."
[Once the saint passes by, the feast is over.]
—Old proverb

— *A behind-the-scenes look at* the people responsible for carrying the feast of Saint Rocco from their small village in Southern Italy to the streets of the North End. Veneration of saints who possessed the power to grant special wishes and to heal the sick was an ancient part of Italian culture, a belief that began with the pagan gods of Magna Grecia in southern Italy and a ritual still practiced by the members of the San Rocco Society.

During my interview with Mary Nastasi, her two grandchildren came in from playing outside. They saw what was going on, sat on her lap, and listened intently as she told me the history of San Rocco.

THE HISTORY OF THE FEAST OF SAINT ROCCO

The feast of San Rocco began in 1921, my parents and their people from the village of San Michele Baronia [provincia di Avellino] brought it here. I remember from when I was five years old how we used to look forward to the feast. We'd all get dressed in our fineries, and after the procession all us kids would go to our hall on Snow Hill Street—all the people would be dancing, our mothers would cook everything from soup to nuts. The cousins would come from all over to visit us—it was one happy family. There was never any bickering, even though money was scarce and wages were low. Everything was cheaper and our mothers used to prepare the tables for everyone—it was a ball.

During World War II they stopped the feast because all the boys were at war, so we just had a procession. In 1949 they started the feast up again and it lasted two days and one night, from Saturday to Sunday. In the old days only the *paesani* [people from the same village in Italy], the people of the society, used to do everything. Their children used to carry the flags, the ribbons, the

◀ Mary Nastasi walking barefoot in the San Rocco procession, 1981

flowers, and carry the saint—but no more. It's kinda hard now—just the men carry the saint down the stairs at the church and sometimes you can't even get them. My cousin Josie dresses up the saint and puts all the gold on him. Then Josie and Jimmy Brovaco take turns watching the saint overnight, and on Sunday I donate the Mass and the procession follows with the Roma Band. But the young generation doesn't bother with it anymore—I don't know why. They come down for the Mass, but they really don't take an interest in it. But, you know, I'm surprised that quite a few people from outside the North End call me—they're from the same town as my parents in Italy—they ask if their nephews and nieces could carry a flag or a ribbon in the procession. I say sure and we let them take turns. It keeps the tradition alive. Up until ten years ago you had to bid to carry San Rocco or to carry the flowers, even the ribbons or the banner. The highest bidder carried it.

I try to keep the feast as religious as possible. I don't know what's happened, but it's getting out of hand—prices have gone way up, the printer charges more, the band costs more, the cost of the food [for everyone in the procession]—it costs a lot. And the city won't help us by picking up the trash bags left behind.

A VOW TO SAINT ROCCO

You try to keep the tradition. Seventeen years ago my daughter had a disease of the arteries in her hand and the doctors wanted to amputate it. I wouldn't let them do it. After I came to my senses, I made a vow that if they wouldn't touch her and if she got better, I would open my house for two days [during the feast] in honor of San Rocco. I vowed to give all the donations to the church and that I would walk barefoot during the procession until the last day I lived. And every year since that day my daughter and I walk the procession together.

To this day they haven't touched her. Like my cousins [the Brovacos], when they have serious problems, they prayed to San Rocco. Could it be or isn't it, the power of San Rocco— you have to wonder. So it has to be if you believe in it, but you have to believe in it real strong. You have to work for it—you have to earn it—you can't pray today and forget for a week and start all over again. You have to pray every day and every night.

{ *Jimmy Brovaco was known in the neighborhood as the official carrier of Saint Rocco. A solidly built man with huge biceps, he bore the responsibility for carrying the 400-pound statue of the saint down a flight of stairs at age seventy-four, with the help of a younger man.* }

CARRYING SAINT ROCCO

I came to America in 1926, but my mother brought me back to Italy when I was two years

▲ Jimmy Brovaco, 1980

old. I came back to America when I was eighteen years old, and it's been my job to carry San
Rocco from the second floor to the first and
then through the streets of the North End for
fifty years. But now I'm getting old and I can't
do it anymore. I just got too old and now
there's no one left to help me.

(translated from Neapolitan dialect)

{ *Never having learned English, Tommasina Brovaco still spoke in Neapolitan dialect when
she was sixty-nine years old. Her voice rose in operatic fashion as she talked about Saint Rocco.* }

ON THE MIRACULOUS POWER OF SAINT ROCCO

We believe that all the saints have miraculous powers, but Saint Rocco is very special to us. And
you have to believe in him. When it was time for my husband's heart operation, he was quite
frightened to have it done. But he had no choice, really. The night before his operation, he had a
dream of Saint Rocco, who told him, "Joe, have the operation and have no fear—I am with you."
The next morning, after the operation was over, my husband told me the story. And he went
through the operation in total peace. And that's why we hold Saint Rocco in such veneration!

(translated from Neapolitan dialect)

▲ Mary Nastasi placing the crown on San Rocco as Tommasina Brovaco holds the cane and
Josephine Bossio looks on

{ *Josephine Bossio was the president of the San Rocco Society who, with her elderly assistants,*
did all the background preparations for the procession and the dressing up of the statue. }

ON BEING HEALED BY THE POWERS OF SAN ROCCO

When I was six years old in Italy, my sister and I had a terrible sickness. And the doctor told my mother that there was nothing that could be done to save us. In desperation my mother went up to our church to pray to Saint Rocco to help us. Our church was on the side of a small mountain overlooking our village below. In those days, when death came to a family in our village, people would scream and cry. My mother, crying and screaming alone up in that church, could be heard all the way down to the village. Alarmed, some of the people ran up to the church, where they found my mother unconscious on the floor. In that moment, my sister and I felt healed, and to this day we thank and honor Saint Rocco for saving us.
(translated from Neapolitan dialect)

▼ The San Rocco Feast, 1980

MAKING WINE

NET WEIGHT 42 LBS.

CHAPTER FOURTEEN

Making Wine

"L'acqua fa male, il vino fa cantare."
[Drinking water is bad, but wine makes one sing.]
—Old proverb

— *One of the traditions brought from* the Old Country was the ancient rite of winemaking. In its North End incarnation, it began with the careful selection of California grapes, called for squeezing from the grapes every last drop of juice, and ended in fermentation in large wooden vats in the cellars of North End apartment houses. In Italian homes homemade wine was considered a natural part of each meal and was respected for its medicinal qualities. One elder who drank wine at daily meals said, "I only drink wine because city water rots the pipes."

I visited Pasquale Capone during each stage of the winemaking process in his cellar, photographing him each day. As we neared the end, he told me stories of Italy and seemed content that another year had passed and the cycle of making wine had been completed.

A LIFETIME OF MAKING WINE

I came from Italy in 1914—no mother, no father, no sister, no money, and no job. I was sixteen years old. Nineteen-twenty was the first year I make-a wine. I make-a only one barrel. I have-a no money—could I make anymore? But now I make-a three or four barrels for my family—my grandachilren like the wine, my daughter, and my son too. I make cause I no like the wine in the store. I no like the store wine. The store wine—that's-a no grape wine. Cause I been in California two times, my son take me to the place where they make the wine, and over there, one barrel was vinegar—33,000 gallons—bigger than my house! I dunno how many kinds of wine they showed me that day. And I never liked one! That's because a chemical is in there, the one you buy in the store, it's a chemical. See, you gotta know the grape, no everyone make the same I make. I know the grape. I know the grape upside down. For sixty years, I make wine. When you buy the grape,

◄ Pasquale Capone

▲ Pasquale Capone in his cellar squeezing grapes with a *stringiatura* [wine press]. It was common for North End homes to have this device cemented into the foundation of their cellars.

soon as you toucha them, the inside comma right out. When I buy 'em, the stuff, when you squeeze 'em, no comen out. And when you put 'em in your mouth, it's gotta crack-a like-a nuts. And it's gotta be a little dry. I know the grape upside down. I pick the best I can do, that's all—that's all I can pick. The grapes I used to buy years ago—they was outta this world. But no more. They don't come here anymore. But I get the best what I can get. I pay more price, that's all. But no more like four or five years ago—forget about that. I dunno where they go, or they usa them down there, I dunno.

Yeah, I be makin' wine sixty-one years this year. I'm eighty-three, all right? This year it costs $12 for thirty-six pounds of grape. Cost me pretty close to $6.00 a gallon. Yep. But I no care, I no wanna stop. I no drink much, I drink two glass a night—depend how I feel. I no drink if I no feel like. If I feel like one glass, I have one glass, if I feel like have-a two, I have-a two. And then it's the next night again.

Whiskey, I didn't touch 'em. That don't agree with me any more. Ha ha! The wine is the most healthy than beer or whiskey . . . unless you overdo. That's no good. If you eat too much it's no good. Like-a me, I drink two glass this night—it'll be the next day again. I never touch anything after this.

A WINEMAKING SESSION WITH PASQUALE

Last night we squeeze the grapes in a machine at my daughter-in-law's house. We leave it in the barrel ten, maybe stay twelve days—dependa how much sugar it has in [the grapes]. If there's a lot of sugar, it boila quick. This here, no gotta mucha sugar, my niece gotta the thing

▲ Pasquale sitting while grapes ferment

to measure how much sugar. And this is what we make-a last night. Take about fifteen minutes to squeeze. Years ago, before I come here, they used the feet—that's all they had, put on
the boots. I used to do it by hand, with a *stringiatura* [a mechanical grape squeezer]. See, I
put all the juice out. It comes up like this when it starts to boil [fermentation], come up like
that. And I come [down the cellar] every night and every day—I got this long thing [a pitch-
fork] and every day I come down and I push 'em [the grapes in the barrel] down. Once a day.
The next day I come in . . . zop! . . . I push 'em down and it stoppa boil. And then stoppa
boil. When it stoppa boil, I tastem . . . when it come out, the sweet gone, I take the juice out
and put in the press and I squeeze little by little—not all at once—give a little bang and let it
go for ten minutes and give another four or five bangs.

THE OLD WAYS

▲ Pinelli family at the table

CHAPTER FIFTEEN

The Old Ways

"La via vecchia non si cambia per la via nuova—sa quello che tiene, ma non sa quello che trova."
[One never changes the old ways for the new—you know what you have,
but you never know what you'll find.]

—Old proverb

— *The elders of the North End* abided by Old World traditions and customs, kept alive and intact until the late 1970s. One reason this Italian-American culture survived so long was due to the neighborhood's geographic isolation from the rest of the city, enforced by an expressway that divided it from City Hall and Government Center, and by a circular strip of waterfront that skirted the neighborhood's periphery. Recognizing that the North End was changing, they spoke eloquently about the stark contrasts between their old ways and the ways of the "New Boston."

I interviewed Helen Luongo sitting at her old-fashioned, porcelain-covered kitchen table. Beside the table was her sewing machine, where she made the brightly patterned curtains for her kitchen windows.

THE LOVE OF THE FAMILY

I would rather have a Depression; I wish we lived the way we were living in those days. People were happy. My mother wouldn't give us cocoa, or coffee, or milk—she'd buy cocoa shells to make cocoa in the morning—she'd make a big pan. Then she'd get the bread and we couldn't have two or three slices of bread—one loaf of bread had to be enough for the whole family—we didn't have . . . but the happiness that we had! The closeness of the family! You don't find that today. You don't find that closeness—that love of the family isn't there anymore. You wouldn't think of sitting down to eat unless the whole family was there—everybody had to be at the table. And you had to sit until everybody was through. This is the way it was in my house.

▲ J&N Market, corner of Prince and Salem

{ *Phil D'ellasandro came from a family of ten children.* }

IT HAD TO BE FRESH

Our folks taught us to thank Almighty God at the beginning and at the end of the day. You always said grace before and after all meals—I don't care, even if you had a cup of coffee, the important thing was to thank God for it—everything comes from the Creator. Once we get away from Him, people begin to stop to think. They can't think of the right direction anymore. People don't seem to have what we had. It was either that you come to my house or I come to yours—we'd sit down—if they were having a meal, well, you'd move the chair over for somebody else. You didn't need a special invitation whether they came to your house. "Come in," they'd say to you. You couldn't leave without eating a good meal and that was a good feature about the good Italo-Americans.

▲ Salem Street meat market with freshly cut goat skins

Rabbits were a favorite in the winter; baked cow head was a delicacy more than anything else. Sweetbreads—we used to call them *mogliadelli* many years ago. With cow hearts, livers we made big stews—it would be a great treat for everyone. You take Easter, you had to have fresh lamb—they wouldn't buy lamb from the chain stores which was frozen out of state or out of town. They had to go to the butcher's shop and it had to be cut in their presence or they wouldn't buy it.

The same thing with poultry. Many years ago there was a poultry shop on Fulton Street—you'd go in and choose your own chicken and they'd kill it, singe the feathers on it. Everything with the Italo-American prior to the '40s had to be fresh, if it wasn't fresh killed or in their presence, they wouldn't buy it. The next generation came along and they couldn't find the time to do those things, to stay home and cook a meal. It wasn't that they didn't have the money—it's the time. Today people don't even have time to bless themselves and say thank God for the day today.

{ *Al Mostone spoke reverently about old-fashioned wakes held in the house, almost as if to say that the old way of paying respect to a departed family member was better than the modern way.* }

WE HAD OUR WAKES IN THE HOUSE

In those days the wakes were always in the house. We never went to an undertaker or an undertaker's parlor. We'd stay up all night with the body. It was all by candles, there was no electricity. That's the way it was, all by candlelight.

{ *Mary Molinari wanted to go to college but was forced to leave school for work. She said, "I swore I would send my sons to college, even if I had to scrub floors—and they both finished."* }

LIFE IN THE OLD APARTMENT HOUSE

We used to go up on the roof on summer nights and my uncle had a guitar, my father had a mandolin, and they'd play together up on the roof. My mother had a table . . . what table? . . . it was a box! She'd put a tablecloth on it, cut up watermelon, peaches, and in a big pitcher we'd have wine and peaches all cut up. You'd think it was a penthouse up there! The place was coming down on us, but we were happy.

We loved each other—people were different then. They were humble in those days. We used to have weddings right in the house. In our house we'd go down to see the people on the second and third floor. We'd visit each other—have coffee. I'd go up and down those stairs two or three times a day, and it was good exercise. Now I've moved to a condo [after being evicted]. But I still liked the old ways better. As you'd walk up, you'd see your neighbor on the different flights of stairs, and we'd have coffee together. But today, these new homes for the elderly are like hotels—all tight and closed. It isn't like years ago. Now everyone watches television inside. Before, it was different, people would leave their doors open and no one was afraid of anything. Someone would always come by to see you—they'd tap on your door and come into your house. In the old building it was one big family. Now everyone locks their doors up, and they have to call before they come to see you. In the old building if they'd hear you going up or down the stairs, they'd come out of their doors and say Hi, good morning, and talk to you so nice. You know what I liked? Years ago, coming out of church, walking down the street, you could smell the sauce coming out of the kitchens for Sunday dinner. We used to enjoy that kind of living. Now when they cook, they've got fans to blow the air out of the kitchen—and all the smell goes out too.

Annie   Rita   Jennie   Madre   Marie   Lena

▲ Arrigo family on the rooftop, 1920s

I used to live on Garden Court Street. The whole street was one big family. Summer nights, we'd all sit together outside—who would buy cantelope, who would buy watermelon—and we'd eat together at night . . . it was like a picnic. We were like brothers and sisters on that street. Today? I feel lost, everything has changed.

> *Frank Favazza vividly recalled that no oil burners or steam heat existed in apartment buildings. People chopped wood for their stoves on the sidewalks because there were no cars. "There was plenty of room to walk and people often sat on the curbs, with their feet dangling in the street—whoever who had a car in those days were considered millionaires," he said.*

CARRYING THE BREAD ON MY HEAD

There was no such thing as going down to the store to get a loaf of bread. My mother used to make the bread dough, and there used to be a bakery on Fleet Street where they used to bake your bread—the baker would say to come back in a couple of hours. And she used to make the round breads, put them on a board—one, two, three—put it on my head. And quite a few times that bread slipped off, the board onto the sidewalk, and I'd pick them up as best I could. But I'm tellin' ya, they'd taste even better—of course, I suppose the streets weren't as dirty as they are now. And my mother would say to me, "What's that dark thing here on the bread?" I'd say, "Well, the oven maybe cooked it more on that side than the other or something." But they knew.

> *Viola Pettinelli told me that she was forbidden by her parents to walk barefoot. One hot day in the summer, she went to the bakery barefoot. Halfway there, her feet began to burn on the sidewalk and she quickly returned home. She vowed never to walk without shoes again.*

TWO PENNIES EACH

My mother, well, she never went to work. There were seven children so she stayed home. She took care of the house, she did all the cooking, all the sewing, all the patching—she was very good at patching, my mother. You could never notice her patchwork. And she did all her washing by hand with the old washboard. We had one Sunday dress outfit, the boys and the girls. And every Saturday night my mother would wash those Sunday clothes and press them and they were all hung up in the corner. Sunday morning, we'd get up, put on our best, and everyone went to the "children's Mass" at 9:00. We all had to go Mass, and my father would give us two pennies each because that's what we put in the collection box—that priest would be glad to get the two pennies, so here was my father near the door, two pennies each, and we'd go off to church Mass on Sunday.

> *Josephine Tranquillo re-created the sense of excitement when her brother left Charlestown by ship for World War I. She described the big band playing, the people singing, "Over there, over there, buy a bond, over there, over there, and we will march on, over there," and cheering to their loved ones as the soldiers waved back. Her brother never returned.*

THE OLD DAYS IN THE OLD APARTMENT

I live in Casa Maria [elderly housing project] now. But I used to live in an apartment house before. You'd go downstairs to see the neighbors standing in front of their doors. And they'd greet you. That meant a lot. Now, today, in my building, you don't see a soul. You push a button, get on the elevator—and there's nobody there. You could drop dead and nobody knows.

The other day my daughter came to my place. So I was making toast and while we were talking, the toast burned, smoke all over the house. So I opened the door to let the smoke out. And nobody came out of their apartment. So I put the fan on, put on the air conditioner, and I finally got all the smoke out. Still and all, no one would come out and ask me what was the matter.

I miss going up and down the stairs in my old building. I miss everything. I miss my rooms, I miss the whole building—I lived there for forty-two years. I had a beautiful flat. Now what do I see from my window? I don't see anything. Where I live now, all I see are rooftops. Who needs that? I see an airplane when it goes by, that's all. What do I see? I see all antennas—all those building antennas. And for some reason they gave me a handicapped apartment—I don't know why—I can dance on my head, I belong to ten clubs. So I said to them [the housing superintendent], "How would you like a handicapped apartment?" She says, "No, I wouldn't." So I said, "So why did you give it to me? I'm never home."

{ *After Paul Grande finished a haircut, the customer stayed in his barber chair and his brother Dominic stood and listened to him tell the following story.* }

THE SICILIAN WOMAN BREASTFED ME

In those days, everybody [in our building] left their doors open. And whoever was sick, everyone would come down—who brought chicken soup, who pressed the clothes, who cooked for you, who made the beds—because the husbands all went to work and they couldn't take care of their wives, so all the neighbors used to take care of them. When my mother died, I was a baby. In those days they only believed in being breastfed. You'd always see women in the street breastfeeding their babies—it didn't bother anyone. You'd walk on the sidewalk and see a woman breastfeeding her child and think nothing of it. And when my mother died, I was a baby—and they didn't have milk bottles or formula or anything like that. So the next door neighbor, the wife of a Sicilian fisherman, breastfed me for two years. And I still know her sons. Everytime I'd see her in the street she'd look at me and say, "How many times I breastfed you!"

THEIR WORD WAS THEIR BOND

There was a closeness in those days, even when they borrowed money. When my father opened his first barbershop in 1904, he had no money in those days. His next door neighbor lent him $300 for a down payment, which in those days was a lot of money. No paper, no note, and they didn't use receipts. Their word was their bond in those days—when they said something, they'd die for it. And, of course, my father paid him back.

COME IN, SEE WHAT I'M COOKING

The milkman didn't like to make deliveries around Christmas or the holidays. Every stop he'd make, people would invite him in, "Have a drink, have a piece of this, have a piece of that." It was impossible to get home sober. Of course, everyone had their own wine—they didn't believe in store-bought wine—and at every stop it was always, "Come in, have some wine, have a cookie." In our building there were six or seven stops, and if they were sitting down eating, they'd say, "Sit down and eat with us." Nowadays, even after two years, people in my building don't even know the people next door. In that sense, the North End has changed. Before, you'd go through a building and all the kitchen doors were open—you could smell the food right in the hallways—it was whatever they were cooking and they'd say, "Come in, see what I'm cooking, taste it."

▲ Paul Grande and his father, 1925

{ *Grace Pinelli was seventy-five at the time of our interview and lived alone.* }

LIFE ISN'T EASY

There was no fear in those days—you felt protected all around you. My mother never had a key for the doors—no doors were locked in the North End. It was neighbor helping neighbor, if a neighbor needed you, you were there—it's not like that now . . . I think life was better

Grace Pinelli (seated at left) with her family ▶

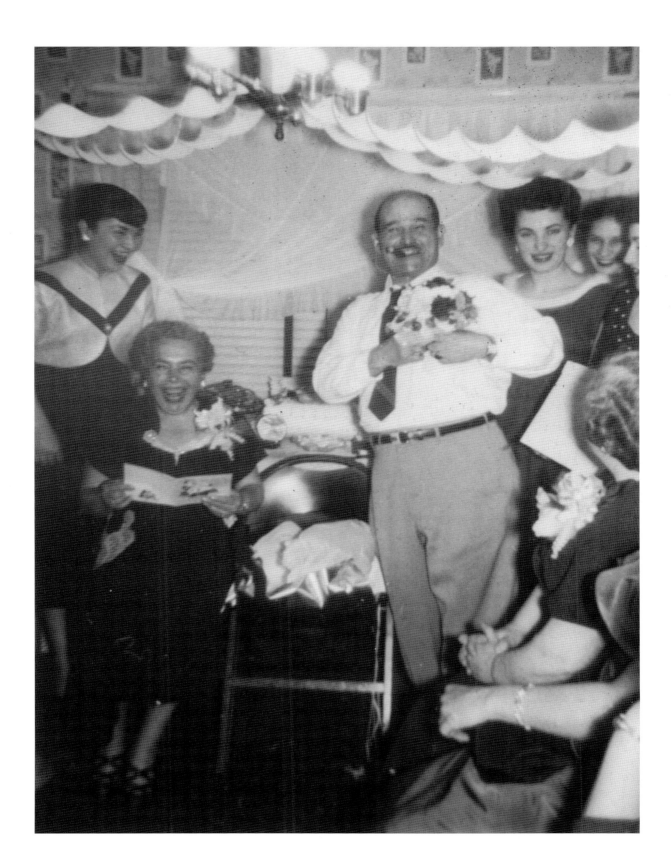

then. Today I'm afraid. I go places only if I have someone with me. You can't have cash in your pocketbook. If you need to buy, you need a checkbook, who needs a checkbook? I don't have that kind of money. So I don't go out that much. I go to the library. On Monday I go to the drop-in center, on Tuesday to my club, Thursday is forum club—that's what I live for. And I look forward to visit my four children. They call me first because there's no place to park and it costs $9.00 or $10.00 to park all day. This [new] apartment has been an extension of my life, every morning I say thank you, Lord. God has been good to me, what have I got to complain about? Life isn't easy. I try to understand my grandchildren. They say, "I want everything, and I want it now." Oooh, I said, it doesn't work that way, life isn't easy.

{ *At the end of our interview, Frances Corolla said, smiling, "I wasn't brought up with riches, I was brought up with love and affection."* }

THE WELCOME SIGN

I had to leave school the second year of high school because the money wasn't enough and my mother needed help. I was working for $7.00 a week. There were eleven of us. We had our chores. We had no time to run out and play. We had to do those chores, and that's how we never got into any mischief. If we had a lollipop we were happy. We lived better then. We were happy. We were all one big family. So if we knew a neighbor was sick, we'd all be there—we'd all run in. Whenever there was sickness, our door was always open—there was always that welcome sign without even knocking on the door.

They'd see you with door open and they'd say, "Come on in," in Italian. "Are you tired?" Or if we had wine, we'd give them a glass of wine or whatever we had on the table we shared—our tables were always full in those days. It was like a welcome sign—you didn't even have to put that welcome on the door because the door was opened. The old people always had that welcome sign—their arms were always open. I knew that if I came home from work late, I wouldn't have to worry about my children—my neighbor would take care of them. And I never forgot that. And that's what I mean about closeness—the love was there. But today it's not so. I miss that—we don't have that today. Today we don't know what's going on or how or when or why.

WE WERE LIKE A CHAIN

We didn't have washing machines then. My mother would get that big pan and put it on the stove and boil—one night you'd soak them, one night you'd boil them, and another night

▲ 1928 class photo, Paul Revere School

you'd put them in bleach. We made our own sausages. My mother made us a lot of polenta with a lot of gravies, homemade macaroni, her own homemade bread—she never went out to buy anything, everything was made in the house. It may sound ridiculous but we enjoyed it. That's all we knew. But now they have dishwashers, and the dryers, and the washing machines—but there isn't that closeness. If my sister was doing the stairs and we couldn't go by the stairs, we'd be doing something else until she'd get through and then we'd do something else—like a chain, we kept very busy, very busy. It's really sad—these kids today, where do they get all that money? But, you know, they're not as clean as us. When I do my stairs in the hallway by hand, the young girl upstairs laughs. She says she never did things like this when she was growing up. I said to her, "I've done this all my life." This is how we were brought up.

In 1919 fourteen-year-old Viola Pettinelli left the eighth grade and began a forty-eight-hour workweek in a book bindery, which she found "fascinating." Being underage, she had to attend Continuation School on North Bennett Street until she was sixteen. She earned $10 a week and considered herself lucky.

THE TEACHER IS YOUR MOTHER

We had nice teachers in those days. Our teachers were dedicated—if they got married, they couldn't be teachers. We had a lot of unmarried teachers, we had elderly teachers—they were terrific. In those days, they went to Radcliffe, Wellesley, and Simmons—and they were terrific. I really miss those teachers. They taught us beautifully—they were beautiful teachers. I liked them all very much, the teacher was always right there. When I was in the third grade, we had one girl who was fresh and the teacher seemed to be having trouble with her. The teacher was a lovely teacher—Mrs. Bibby, an older teacher with beautiful white hair and she had red and white skin, she had a pretty, chubby face. She asked this girl to take her mother in and the girl never told her mother, so the teacher sent another girl to the house to tell the mother that she wanted to speak to her. So this woman, nice, tall woman, came to school with a baby in her arms. She comes in and the teacher calls another pupil to interpret for her. When the mother hears what was told to her [about her daughter], she took the baby out of her arms, put the baby on the front desk—her daughter was standing nearby. Well, she slapped that girl's face—oh, the girl was highly embarrassed. We were all embarrassed for her. We all got our slaps, but right in the classroom in front of all the kids! And the teacher just looked on. Then the mother took the baby and said to the teacher, "All right, all right, if she gives you any more trouble" . . . and she left.

We weren't supposed to give any teachers or priests or nuns any trouble. No back talk. My mother, when we went to school, she said, "When you're in school, the teacher is your mother." That's the way we were brought up. You couldn't go home and say so-and-so hit me. My parents would ask, "And why did she hit you?" "He hit me for nothing," we'd say. So everytime you'd say you did nothing wrong, you'd get a whack in the face. "You stayed after school?" "Why?" "I did nothing." Bang! "What did you do?" "Nothing!" Bang! You'd get another one. Until you told your mother what you did. Because no mother would believe that a teacher was going to keep you after school for nothing.

Discussing politics on a North End street corner, 1980 ▶

LOCAL POLITICS

▲ Elderly protest march, 1981

CHAPTER SIXTEEN

Local Politics

"A do' cantano tanti galli, non fa mai il giorno."
[Whenever too many roosters crow at the same time, the dawn never comes.]

—Old proverb

— *By the 1970s city politics* had become a fact of life for the people of the North End. The old system of community self-reliance to solve its problems was replaced by a "Little City Hall," a satellite agency of City Hall and the Kevin White administration, which was staffed by political appointees of the mayor whose main task was to deliver votes at election time.

Fred Bourne chuckled when he described how much money he made during the Depression, earning a dollar for every sailor he delivered to a local brothel. "My wife helped feed everyone on Unity Street," he said with a laugh. Fred had a great sense of how Boston politics worked on the local level.

THE RISE OF THE ITALIAN POLITICIAN

The Irish were mostly politicians—including President Kennedy's grandfather, John F. Fitzgerald ["Honey Fitz"]—and many other Irish families. You see, for years Ward 3, The West End and The North End, was dominated by the Irish even though in later years the Italians became the biggest percentage of the people living in the North End. It used to be politicians like George Lannigan, John F. Fitzgerald, and the Lomazney brothers—what they used to do was put up nine Italian candidates, pay for their campaigns, and one Irishman, so that the Italian vote would be split up nine ways and the Jewish and the Irish vote would elect the representative to the City Council for Ward 3. In fact, one time they even put up a Jewish dentist for representative—Doctor Finkelstein—and he got elected [laughs]. In an Italian district!

The North End became a kind of melting pot for the Italian immigrant as the Jews with money moved to West Roxbury and the Italians to Medford. They began to do well in the construction business, and they began buying their own homes in the North End. As the Italians moved in and they had children and their children became Americanized, they wanted representation, so Joseph Langone ran for state senator, and he was the first Italian from the North End to achieve political prominence and, of course, his sons inherited the mantel from the father because he became so well-known. And others followed and won elections. And this is how the Italians evolved politically and how they finally got representation.

> *Phil D'ellesandro held many positions of honor in the community, becoming a Grand Knight in the Knights of Columbus and a chief organizer of community activities. He was seventy-seven at the time of our interview.*

POLITICS IN THE NORTH END

We used to have our own volunteer committees that dealt with issues like rubbish pickup, traffic direction. We took records of cars parked [illegally], and we used to help the Italian-speaking people with their bills when they couldn't understand. I was one of the original community advocates to set in motion the "Rehabilitation Program" assigned to address community problems. It's not our generation anymore, although we tried to set a good example. And the whole idea of the Little City Hall evolved out of our work. The stuff we used to do for nothing—they're getting paid for, seven or eight people doing nothing, calling it a Little City Hall!

> *When Michelina Manfra ended her story, there was an unmistakable smile of satisfaction on her face, having kept her mayoral vote a secret. Despite being pressured to vote for Mayor White, she never disclosed whom she actually voted for in the mayoral election.*

COERCED TO VOTE FOR THE MAYOR

Richie, the one who works for Mayor White, came to the park looking for me. He wanted to know who I was voting for. He says to me, "Who you voting for?" And I said to him, "I dunno, maybe for nobody!" He say-a to me, "Oooh no—you gotta vote-a for Mayor White!" I say-a to him, "Maybe yeah, eh maybe no!" "Oh no, you gotta do-a for me," he say. I say Richie, I like-a you, I know Richie from when he was a smalla boy, you know? I say, "I like-a you—maybe I no gonna vote per [for] no one!" "Oh no, you gotta vote-a for me, you gotta vote-a for the Mayor White." He said, "I no make-a you go there [to vote], I come-a to you house and you vote-a you house." I said, "Oh no, I go a vote at the Michelangelo school." He say, "No, I bring-a the paper [an absentee voter form] home eh you vote inna your house because I make-a sure that you . . ." "So I say [voice rising], "Look-a, Richie, iffa you say I gotta vota for Mayor White, eh you gotta come-a to my house and make-a me vote, I no vote-a for no one!" He getta mad. So I said, "All right, I'm gonna vote-a for Mayor White." So when I went to vote, who do I find over there? Richie! Like-a this [grimaces], with a long face! When I go in there [to vote], nobody know for who I vote— I never tell-a for who I vote. You know who I vote for? I vote for the one who comes out [wins the election]! Whoever come out—I vote-a for him. If he no come out, I no vote-a for him—I voted for the other one. Is it his [Richie's] business who I vote for?

Helen Luongo paused several times during this interview as a way of paying homage to the old traditions.

POLITICS AND SAINT ANTHONY

Now look at all this trash he's [mayor] doing to our feasts. We didn't have this trash that we have now with our feasts. Are there North Enders at these feasts? Is there the tradition that we had? These feasts were something that came in from our great-grandfathers—brought it over here [tapping finger on the table]. The Saint Anthony feast? Why, my father, my husband used to go crazy when the feasts came—it was a big deal! It was a tradition. There was something behind it. But now, what is it? What do they have? All these trailers and pushcarts that come from all over—from Connecticut, from Rhode Island, from New York, from New Jersey. It's a racket, a racket. There's no more tradition behind it. Why? . . . Why? Do you know why? It's Mayor White advertising it as "Summerthing." All right? Even that he took away from us. Even that he took away from us down here. He advertises it as "Summerthing" on the radio, in the newspapers, on the television, and everything.

   And you got the swill. They don't know the meaning behind our feasts. In Montefalcione—my father's village—they used to buy a baby pig—it belongs to the town—and that pig is taught to go from door to door eating every day—everybody feeds him. On this day, Saint Anthony's Day, they raffle off that pig and that's how they pay for the fireworks and whatever they have. And that's what they call *'o porco di Sant'Antonio* [the pig of Saint Anthony]. Yeah, *'o porco di Sant'Antonio*—you go eating from house to house, and that's the meaning, and as a child I couldn't understand it when my parents used to say, *"Eh, oggi si fa la festa dello porco di Sant'Antonio."* [Today is the feast of the pig of Saint Anthony]. And then as I grew I saw the tradition that was behind it. In Italy the highest bidder carries the banner of Saint Anthony in the procession.

   They [The Society] used to make money before, but it was given for good purposes—for scholarships, some to the church, they'd give some to organizations like the Home for Italian

Children, to MS, to the cancer organizations. Now what do they do with all that money they make? I don't believe in it anymore. There used to be people who'd come from Philadelphia, from New Jersey, from New York, from Pennsylvania down here—for this day, Saint Anthony's. They don't come down anymore because they see the swill that goes on. The meaning of the day has gone out of it. Before "Summerthing" started, Saint Anthony wouldn't come by my door without me giving money. Now since it's gone this way I don't give them a penny, to any of them. Because they could've stopped it—even though "Summerthing" advertises it and they send a band down to play—if they didn't want it, they could've stopped it. Let's keep our tradition! What is it, *Fiddler on the Roof?* Tradition! Oh, I think he's [the mayor] done worse to the North End than what they did to the West End. At least those people, they knocked their houses down and they had to get away—but we have our houses standing over here and he's squeezing us out of our houses. This is it. We have no say. The only thing you can do is pack up and move away.

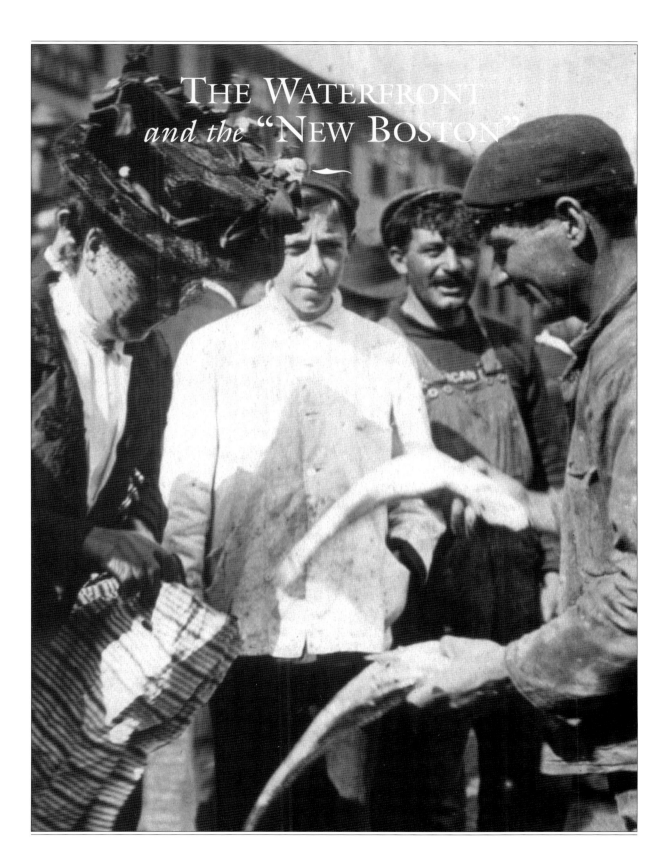

THE WATERFRONT
and the "NEW BOSTON"

View of Boston Harbor from Commercial Street

CHAPTER SEVENTEEN

The Waterfront and the "New Boston"

— *In the mid-1970s urban planners* transformed the North End's Waterfront section from a blighted, vermin-infested area of abandoned warehouses and crumbling docks that no Bostonian would dare visit into a new neighborhood of expensive waterfront condominiums, handsome hotels, fancy restaurants, and trendy bars. The Waterfront area and its most famous tourist attraction, Faneuil Hall, were once a nerve center of the Northeast, with railways, warehouses, and busy unloading docks that handled and distributed goods to cities and towns throughout New England. The new Waterfront attracted upwardly mobile professionals and drew millions of tourists each year; it also represented the split in the North End between two societies: the old Italian neighborhood on fixed incomes and the modern neighborhood of the new ethnics.

When Al Mostone re-created scenes of the Waterfront at the turn of the century, the flow of his words had the power to convey what it was like to be in the midst of a busy commercial center in its heyday.

ON THE WATERFRONT IN 1915

I worked as a newspaper boy and shoeshine boy on Atlantic Avenue on the Waterfront. I used to board the ships—the *North Star,* the *Calvin Austin*—I was allowed to go on the ships and I'd leave papers for the captains, the mates, the crewmen . . . as a matter of fact I used to have my suppers there onboard ship.

I'd shine shoes for them, and if they had suits, I'd take them to the tailor, then take it back to them. We had a lot of cafes on the avenue, and in these cafes we had a lot of "sporting women." Well, when they were broke and I'd be at the train entrance at State Street, they'd come up to me and say, "Al, I need 25 cents"—so I'd give them 25 cents, and then, when they'd come out with their gentlemen friends, they'd always double what they gave me. So I was doing pretty good earning $5.00, $6.00 a week. I was seven when I started until thirteen. Atlantic Avenue was mostly stores, fish markets on the wharf side of the avenue, and on the opposite side there was a market, but most of it is gone.

All the farmers used to bring their produce to this market on North and South Market Street—that's where they used to deliver and that's where all the terminals were at that time. I used to sell 1,500–2,000 papers a night because of all the coffee shops nearby. They'd roast the coffee right there. There were nut-roasting stores and liquor warehouses, offices. The Custom House was there, and the people used to come down to that area because Rowe's Wharf used to have the ferry boats going to Revere and Nantasket, and people used to come down to State Street and go downstairs to take the streetcars to East Boston. We had the Union freight lines—that brought in business—they used to transfer the freight cars all through Commercial Street—all the way as far as South Station.

They used to transfer the freight cars into the different wharves, Union Wharf, Lewis Wharf. There were people working in these warehouses. We had the Lincoln Powerhouse that supplied all the electricity for the North End and parts of Boston. We had the "elevated," which started at North Station, a shuttle which ran all the way to South Station—it would take people to South Station and from there they took trains to whatever towns they lived in. Everything was horse and wagon. The Sicilian fishermen . . . most of the Sicilian people were in the fish business and they had their own private boats. They used to all come in at Long Wharf, T Wharf, Eastern Packet Pier. And they all lived in the North End. And then, the people they'd sell the fish to had stores and shops all along Atlantic Avenue on the wharf side. And there were bar rooms, tobacco stores—they had everything at the time, all on one side. We had warehouses, and quite a few roasting houses for nuts, coffee all the way up to Washington Street.

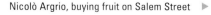

Nicolò Argrio, buying fruit on Salem Street   ►

{ *Charlie Polcari, who had a lemonade stand on the Waterfront in the 1920s, re-created* }
how New York's Waterfront overtook Boston's in size and importance.

WHEN BOSTON WAS SLEEPING, NEW YORK WAS AWAKE

On Wednesdays and Fridays they had a line of people for buying fish. For 25 cents you'd get twenty-five pounds of fish. One time they [fishermen] gave me a basket and I couldn't even carry it home. A lot of my friends used to work down there [on the Waterfront] for 35 cents an hour. Maybe fifteen fellas all line up to unload the bananas from the ships—you hand it to me and I hand it to you, till you got all the way up the street. That's how they got the bananas out of the boats. Bananas. There used to be a man who'd come around on the corner and sell thirteen bananas for 10 cents. Today you pay 40 cents for one or two! You know what they say? *"Acqua passare non passano piu il molino."* You know what that means? The time went by and now there's no more grain to be ground—that's what the old world's saying.

All the ships from Europe—from Italy, France—they used to land in Charlestown. What happened? When Boston was sleeping, New York was awake. You know what they did? They built a big port in New York so the ships wouldn't come here anymore. You should've seen all the stuff

▼ Fishermen selling fish on the waterfront

▲ Overview of Commercial Street, 1900

that the Italian people used to buy when they'd go back to the Old Country—clothing, everything. They used to buy to bring to the Old Country for presents. When the ships started to go
to New York, all the Jewish businessmen [storeowners] around here went out of business. In
1924 when Boston was sleeping, New York was awake. I used to see the Italian and French ships
coming in because I used to cross the bridge at Chelsea to go to work. After they built the port
in New York, the people said, "Yeah, when Boston was sleeping, New York was awake."

▲ 1980 photo of same scene showing changes

Mary Molinari, a lifelong resident of the North End, was harassed by her landlord to move and eventually was evicted. She was grateful to Jim Amalfitano, who helped her find an alternative place to live.

THE WATERFRONT'S EFFECTS ON SMALL STORES

Faneuil Hall, which was part of the development of the Waterfront, made the taxes go up a lot in the North End. And a lot of things go on down there—it's a disgrace—they get drunk, they sleep in doorways. A lot of people get robbed down there. They should do something. They think everyone who lives on the Waterfront is rich, but they don't understand that a lot of them [elderly] had to vacate their apartments and were moved there—and they're living there by the skin of their teeth, let's put it that way. Some of the little stores [in the neighborhood] have been going out of business because of the big stores—the big ones eat the little ones and it's a shame.

▲ Boarded up stores on Salem Street, 1980

Now I'll be frank with you—I don't go in the big stores, I'd rather go in the little stores because those same people gave us a lot of happiness way back—why should I let them go out of business? Let the rich stay with the rich ones. Let the big stores stay by themselves—they can afford it, but the little ones—they can't. Now since they built the Quincy Market, a lot of stores have gone out of business. They used to have Christmas lights outside the stores on Salem Street—no more. I noticed two or three on Salem Street went out of business, they can't—they've been hittin' 'em one after another . . . I do all my shopping on Salem Street. I know the people. Let them live. I can't see all the big stores . . . it's a pity. I feel sorry for those people.

The A&M fruitstand and vegetable store on Causeway Street in 1981—one of the last in the North End ▶

{ *Frances Corolla predicted that within five years "the North End will be gone." She was referring to the old neighborhood people who gave the North End its soul.* }

WE WERE UNITED

I used to go down to the North End Park on the Waterfront—we used to have the salt water. I used to bring my children down there every day. People came from all over—we never had any problems. Jewish people came, coloreds used to come, Italians used to come—we were all united. We used to have a good time at that park. The kids would always be around you, you'd sit with a certain group of friends, they'd wait for you. We used to have a floating hospital for sick children that would take them away for the day. We used to have fireworks. I don't like the change. I'd rather the old way. It was more homey. Now it's for the people who can afford it. It's people like us who can't afford it. The condominiums coming up—I think that's bad—they're moving us out. This is our home. They just want to push the Italian people out. I think it's sad. And to buy a condo? Why put yourself in debt? You're having a hard time just paying your rent now and they're going up and every time you turn around, everything is going up. It's a beautiful place, yes, but I'd rather have the old place. We were more united, more close. This way, we're not close. Down the Waterfront, they think they're better than you, which they're not, because we've all been born and brought up together.

▼ The North End Park in the 1920s

A NEIGHBORHOOD *in* TRANSITION

▲ The Arrigo family on Sheafe Street, 1930s

CHAPTER EIGHTEEN

A Neighborhood in Transition

— *When Boston's urban planners decided* to demolish and rebuild the Waterfront, it helped stimulate a movement among planners in other American cities to develop and convert abandoned waterfront areas into tourist attractions. As local newspapers hailed the arrival of the "New Boston," affluent professionals discovered the North End to be a safe neighborhood in walking distance of Boston's financial district, and a reverse exodus from the suburbs back to the city ensued. With fancy condominiums overlooking Boston Harbor selling at unheard-of prices, a series of subsidized elderly homes were built for many of the 3,000 neighborhood elders who lived on fixed incomes in old-fashioned, cold-water flats. As elders left their old walk-up apartments for new housing, or were displaced and forced to leave the neighborhood, their dwellings were quickly converted to condominiums that few old-timers could afford.

Rose Giampaola was seventy-three at the time of our interview and lived with her husband in subsidized elderly housing. She explained the housing crisis in the North End.

THE CHANGING HOUSING MARKET

Because the landlords are renovating their apartments and the new people are moving in, the old apartments as they were before, the rents used to be $60–$70 for, say, three or four rooms. But when these apartment houses get bought over by a new landlord, the families are put out, they renovate, they do put in bathrooms and heat—but then the rents jump from $60–$70 to $250–$300. They'll put a bathroom in—maybe panel it a little bit, which makes it more livable—but they're getting a big difference in rent. The people in the neighborhood resent people coming in—strangers—because the North End has always been a very ethnic community of all Italians. Now that's changed. I believe it's only 40 percent Italian now. The new people are different, they have a different outlook—it's not the same anymore. In five or ten years the Italian people won't be here anymore because they cannot afford to pay the high rents. Today some landlords are willing to sell their property because they can get a high price for it, but those old tenants have to leave with the new landlords. And, of course, those places [old cold-water flats] get renovated and new tenants come in. And so the tenants—people from the suburbs who are used to paying a higher rent because they already work in the city of Boston—they don't mind paying and they will stay. But the old tenants cannot pay. And we haven't got enough elderly housing for those elderly who have to move because their buildings are being sold. Some of them are fortunate enough to get elderly housing, but not many. We need more elderly housing for the elderly poor in the North End.

Josie Picadacci, in her unassuming, simple way of speaking, measured neighborhood changes by the number of families left in its homes. She told me how she played "amateur hour" with her children "to keep them out of trouble," giving them little prizes, which she wrapped, for the best performance.

THE CHANGING NEIGHBORHOOD

The old people died, a lot of people moved out because they wanted bigger houses. The new people started coming in. Some of them are friendly—I have some living two doors from me in my building, a lot of strange girls—but they're very friendly—they say hi to us when we're outside. When they go by they're friendly—but nothing like it used to be. There aren't homes in North End anymore—it's all single people—young girls, young fellas, whatever—there's no families—they're not giving the places to families anymore. They're not building—it's all apartments for young people. They're not homes.

Though she was seventy-two and in poor health, Rose Amato volunteered regularly at the drop-in center, taking phone calls.

LIFE IN A COLD-WATER FLAT

The lock on my door is broken. My door is opened all night and I live on the ground floor, two steps down. I asked my landlord to fix it. I'm afraid someone may come in. I stay awake at night in the chair because I might hear someone come in. They break in, but she [the landlady] says she isn't gonna fix it. My apartment is very, very cold. I want to get out. There's no bath—I have to go to my daughter's to take my showers. Any day now the plaster in my bathroom is going to fall down and hit me. And the toilet still has a pull chain! I'm seventy-two years old. I'm ashamed to bring people there [my flat] although it's spotless. The windows are broken. The electrical wires are connected in the hallway and that's illegal. When I say it's freezin', it's freezin'. One time I had my granddaughter here to sleep in with me. The next day she said, "Grandma, please, no more!" Do you know how many quilts on my bed? Last year I got pneumonia so bad because of the cold. I'm in the basement so I don't get any heat from below, I give it to the people upstairs. The floors are cold. I gotta put on woolen socks and wear them around the house, a long nightgown—pajamas—I don't know how many blankets I have to put on at night. My daughter just gave me two more blankets—she crochets them for me. Gotta lot of blankets, yeah. As I say, I don't mind it because I'm over my daughter's during the day. But if I had to go home and stay there!

I want to go to the Waterfront [elderly housing] or the Casa Maria [same], but I wasn't accepted. A lot of people weren't accepted. My landlady is elderly. She lives alone—she has no one. To keep warm I stay at my daughter's. The rent here is $50, but that's all it's worth. I got three rooms but one is dark, no window—it's only two rooms. I had a health inspector come down and he said, "This is wicked"—he found faults everywhere—but they still haven't called me [for housing]. And I still take care of the building. I listen for people in the hallway, I clean the stairways, I dust all the dirt. I can't even paint the windows because they are so bad. The bathroom walls are all cracked. When it's zero weather, my daughter wouldn't let me stay here because of the time I got pneumonia [from being so cold in my apartment]. I'm doing her [the landlady] a favor to live here. And she went to the Rent Control to ask for more money! They told her I was doing her a favor to live here—they said she was lucky that people were living in the house. When someone comes in the building, the door stays open—I gotta go out and close the door. I use the stove for heat. One side is the oven to cook and I leave it on or—you want me to freeze to death? I put it on high, but I don't feel anything. You can have it high as hell and you can't feel it. I had a plant on my bureau in my bedroom. Guess what? I noticed all the leaves were drooping—it was ice! The leaves were all full of ice and the plant died on me. The heat doesn't make it into the bedroom.

{ *During this interview, Helen Luongo showed me her sewing work, which she had done for thirty-six years. "I sell most of my drapes to people out of town," she said.* }

IT REMINDS ME OF AN INSTITUTION

Those stairs! How much lumber I carried up those stairs [to her apartment]. And now they tell me to get rid of it, get rid of my house! I couldn't get rid of it—where am I gonna go? Three or four people have suggested—why don't you sell your house and go to elderly housing. I tell you the God's honest truth—I don't want them—they remind me too much of an institution. When you go into those apartments, all you see is a small hallway, doorways on each side, everyone is with a key in their hand and they're going into their apartments. That's what you see in an institution—the doors are all locked—you meet people in the hallways you don't know, you meet people in the elevators you don't know. You don't even know who lives in the building. Maybe because I'm so used to livin'. . . Maybe I'm old-fashioned, from the old school. Maybe I'm behind the times.

Frank Favazza, at seventy-eight, was the oldest of eleven children, the only one left in the North End. Many had moved to Gloucester. Frank thought the idea of taping someone's voice was a great way to document a person's life. "What would it have been like if they had tape recorders at the time of Christ?" he asked just as we began taping.

THINGS ARE CHANGING TOO FAST

▲ Portrait of Frank Favazza

I loved the North End. I was born on North Street, and out of eleven children I'm the only one left—all the others are out of town. With the coming of these condominiums the other day—sometimes you can live in a section and you don't go down that street and it's only a three-minute walk. The section I'm talking about is North Square, near Saint Stephen's Church. I noticed the other day a sign, CONDOS! Condominiums, my God! I thought there wasn't such a thing as condominiums, and now I hear they're making condos a stone's throw from where I'm living. They're renovating some buildings—eventually they'll sell the buildings and we'll have to get out. What do they do? They convert them to condominiums. That's what I'm afraid of, that whatever few remain of the Italian population—between dying and not being able to pay the rent . . . well, it's tough.

I tell you, I used to be a fisherman. I used to leave my house [on Hanover Street, where the post office is now], I'd go down to the wharves at any time because we had no set hours like a factory. I'd walk down Richmond Street down to the Waterfront—the Waterfront, not as it is now. I wasn't stopped once, not even somebody asking for a match. Now as soon as it gets dark, even on my own block, I don't go out anymore. I'm afraid. It's been done you

▲ Condo sign

know, but people don't talk about it—they shove you in a doorway and . . . or else . . . or else. They shove you in a doorway and what can you do?

I cannot grasp all the changes in the last few years. And the wharf where we used to tie up our boats had at least fifty or more boats. Now there isn't one left. Things change for one reason or another. Things are changing too fast. And when I lost my old wharf where the new Waterfront is now, that's where all the old-timers like me would congregate on sunny, nice days, talk, and I used to enjoy it. Now, where am I gonna go?

> *Viola Pettinelli said she felt like a "prisoner of fear" in the North End because her friends were afraid to go out. She described the old neighborhood as "vivacious" because people used to go out and walk.*

We Can't Walk Anymore

I liked it better before. I enjoyed my youth in the North End—I enjoyed it very much. I don't think I'd want to change it for something else. I really liked everything about it—in those days, there was more togetherness—we talk about togetherness—no, we had had more togetherness then. We were more safe. Of course in those days I don't think anybody had crime—you could open your windows, your fire escape windows, and nobody bothered. You could go to bed with the windows open. But crime has gotten worse now. It was more vivacious before—we

▲   Fishing pier in the North End with sailboats and condominiums

went out! Now it seems everybody is afraid and nobody wants to go out. Sometimes I say, why
don't we all go out together, three or four of us and go out. Why only go out when we have
a feast? Why can't we go out and take a walk? But nobody does it. And that's sad, that's very
sad. You know what I really miss? Before when it was safe—after you had your supper—you'd
go out with a friend, or even alone, we'd take a walk around the block, we'd go up to Scollay
Square [now Government Center]—that was supposed to be a bad place—nobody ever
harmed us. We went to Scollay Square everytime we had 15 cents to buy an ice cream soda.
There was an old-fashioned ice-cream parlor with the old-fashioned chairs, have your ice cream
and come home. By 10:00 you'd be home—it was nice. Today they say you can't even go up
to Government Center unless there's a big shindig going on—and then they say the old Scollay Square was bad. I don't think it was so bad, there were bad people, but they didn't bother
nice people. Nobody bothered nice people. I miss those days, just to go out some night. We'd
have these hot nights, we'd have our supper, wash the dishes, it would be so nice to take a nice
walk around the block or go up the street and down the street and then go home.

Gregorio and Caterina Lomanno, tenants of a small apartment on Henchman Street, 1980 ▶

OUT *in the* STREET

▲ Josephine Bosco at the time of her eviction, 1980

CHAPTER NINETEEN

Out in the Street

"Prima che conosce una persona, bisogna mangiare un sacco di sale."
[Before you can really know someone, you have to eat a bushel of salt.]

—Old proverb

— *Seeking substantial profits* in the real estate market, North End landlords and outside speculators converted hundreds of outdated apartments into luxury condominiums, which signaled the end of neighborhood stability for the elderly population who subsisted on meager monthly Social Security checks. The upheaval in the housing market severed bonds of trust between tenants and landlords, transforming the old sense of community into a relic of the past.

{ *Josephine Bosco, despite her serious physical ailments and the added burden of facing eviction, kept her sense of humor. She told me that when she died, her children were going to put sponges all around her casket because she kept her apartment so clean.* }

WHAT'S GOING ON IN AMERICA?

Pretty soon, they're gonna throw everyone out in the North End, just like they did in the West End. And I keep my place clean. And he [my landlord] knows. He said, "You've been a good tenant, but I want to make condominiums, so you'll have to get out." And I've been so used to it here—the park out in front here with kids playing all day. When I don't go out, I sit here and watch the kids playing. I've been here forty-two years. I'm seventy-seven years old and . . . I gotta go lookin' for rooms at my age? And I don't feel too hot . . . I've had two eye operations, they found a spot on my lung, then they took part of my lung out—but, OK, there was no cancer. I've got diabetes too. I asked my son, I said, "Come live with me, son, I need you at my age, I'm a widow and I'm alone." I've got no shower, my stove is my heat. If I get a shower, it'll cost me more. Last Monday the landlord came here, "Mrs. Bosco, I've got to tell you something—I'm gonna make these houses into condominiums—if you want to stay and buy it, buy it." He says the most it will be twenty-five or thirty thousand. He says ten thousand down and . . . he thinks the money is like peanuts, the money comes like his money! He's got loads of money. God bless him!

But don't throw people out! For what? For that greenback, for what they're doin'? They're throwing poor people out of . . . where am I gonna go lookin for rooms? The North End won't be the same Little Italy—they're bouncin' us out one by one. They fix a place over a little and they make their money. That's what it is. Last night in bed I kept thinking and thinking, "Where am I gonna go, what am I gonna do?" I am so used to this house, this was my little castle, you know? Forty-two years I lived here—it's nothing for them to say go away. It's airy, it's sunny, this place. I'm attached to it, I'm so attached to it. I don't think I'll find another place like this because I'm so used to this house. I had five children here. And now in my old age, they're throwing me out. When he [the landlord] said it, I was stunned. I give myself the needle for diabetes every day. I've got glaucoma—my son has to put the drops in my eyes—there's a lot of tension in the back. I can't sleep at all at night. For the owners, it's easy for them to throw us out. It seems like a dream—I think I'm dreaming—I don't think . . . I think it's a dream, all a dream. The other night I couldn't sleep—I slept maybe an hour or two, but last night I couldn't shut one eye. I feel lousy today on account of that. I got up cause I was nervous in bed—and the diabetes—so I took a little chocolate, I thought maybe the chocolate would let me fall asleep . . . but . . . I couldn't sleep. See, it's easy for these owners, it's easy. And they're making money too, on the poor people. It's a shame. It's a shame what's going . . . what's going on in life? In my days, it was beautiful. There was respect. For your parents, there was respect. Everything was so lovely. Today, I dunno what's going on in America, it's not the same . . . it's not the same anymore. I'm sorry for my grandchildren and my great-grandchildren. Wouldn't you feel sorry if this happened to your mother—if they did that to her?

Lucia Petringa was sixty-seven at the time of our interview.

DON'T THROW THEM OUT

I was born in the West End. I saw it all torn down. I go by that West End now and I see all those new buildings and I could cry for how many people lived there, owned their own little house and thought they were set for life. Now they're scattered like refugees. I met an elderly widow on Salem Street who lived in the West End. She thought she was all set, owning her house and collecting rents. They forced her out and she had to accept a pittance—she didn't know where to go. All her children were married. The last time I saw her she landed on a fifth-floor apartment on Salem Street [in the North End]. She took a fall all the way down the stairs and she was wearing a surgical collar—she could hardly talk. I felt like crying, I said to her, *"Coraggio, che puo fa?"* [Have courage, what can you do?] She said, "Lucy, I can hardly talk." But you don't see these

▲ Michael Daleo on Parmenter Street

things in the paper, you don't read these things—nobody gives a damn. As long as they [developers] get their money and they build the Longfellow Towers and the Charles Street Complex [highrises in the West End replacing the old apartment houses], they don't care. We lived here in the North End for thirty years, nobody bothered us and they were glad to have us as tenants. Now they take a chance on "transients"—people who work at Government Center, Massachusetts General Hospital, and don't need their cars to save gas. They don't even put up curtains, the new people. All kinds of guys come in to visit these single girls. And the landlords don't care. I don't object to anyone coming into the North End, but you don't throw out families just for the sake of the almighty dollar. All right, I want money too, but there should be a limit. There should be a way to stop these greedy people. I don't know how these people who don't know the language, I don't know how they do it, the poor things—and they're old. I look at these people who don't know the language and I say—boy, do they kick them around—raise their rents. Those people go hungry to pay their rents. And just for the sake of these transients.

TENANTS AT WILL

When you're young, you're not afraid of anything. When you're older, whether you like it or not, there's a limit to your capabilities. And then you don't know the language. And then they have all these cockamamie rulings like "tenant at will." What do these people know about tenant at will? They don't know. In my last apartment, my landlord withheld registering our rents at the Rent Board and registered the house under "rehabilitation." He evicted everyone in our building—remodeled the apartments—got double the rents. You know where those old people ended up? Nursing homes. They lived a few years. Dead. All they needed was that last blow. And do you know how they evicted us—even though we were under rent control? He [the landlord] paid someone to take us off rent control. The story made the *Boston Globe* spotlight, his name and the guy he paid off. But the Italian people are a proud people. If a landlord says move, they move. Now you and I know there are laws here to protect us against landlords taking advantage, to stop them from doing it. All those elderly people, I used to say to them, "Come with me to the Rent Board, we'll all get together." But when it came time they'd say, *"Oh, non mi sento buona"* [I'm not feeling well]. All these elderly tenants have no lease. They're all "tenants at will."

STREET CONVERSATION BETWEEN TWO ELDERLY TENANTS

Woman 1: Sixty dollars more! Did your landlord raise you?
Woman 2: Not yet.
Woman 1: The one who got raised, she lives in her [landlord's] house, but she's moving to elderly housing.
Woman 2: She'll raise it [the rent] again, they always do—my landlord.

Woman 1: Who?

Woman 2: My landlord. My brother just got raised twenty bucks.

Woman 1: And they're supposed to be friends.

Woman 2: I know, forget about friends, friends are the worst ones!

Woman 1: Today especially, it's all money.

Woman 2: It's all money—right!

Woman 1: Money, money, money.

Woman 2: Money first, and then friends.

{ *Rosa Birra was eighty-one and was living alone at the time of this interview.* }

ON BEING EVICTED

I've been here for sixty-two years in the North End. I was twenty years old when I came from the Old Country—all my life I spend in the North End. Now the [owners] people no

▼ Rosa Birra at the time of her eviction notice in 1981

need the house, they sell the house—they give the house to the children. You don't leave me, please! Don't leave me! Remember to help me, all right? Yes, mama, please! That's funny when you have nobody—don't you think so? I laugh but my heart a-cry. Because that's funny, specially when I go to bring the rent money to her [landlady]—$150, she says, "You find anything [rooms] when you looked?" What do you want me to do, I told her, throw me out into the street? No, I won't go. For you, I go in the street? I will not! No! I know the laws. They [owners] eight years ago come from . . . they gotta lot of money. They bought the old shack and now they throw everybody out. They think they do what they want. You gotta wait till I'm ready. You don't have to throw me out. The law protect me, but every time I pay the rent they get me nervous. They say, "When? When? When?" "When-a the time reach"—that's the way I answer—I know what I gotta say to them . . . but . . . huuh . . . what am I gonna do? I don't feel so good anyway. When I get nervous—the more nervous I get, the more bother me, my breathing because I suffer with my heart and the high blood pressure bother me. That's all. The nervous go together and make-a me feel . . . bad. I'm eighty-one years old and I go eighty-two next October. I'm an old person, my dear child, see? I gotta see what I gotta do. If I move from my house—I don't want to move anymore—then I'm gonna move when God-a move me. That's all I wanna do. I try to do my best. So, thank God, still I try to help myself. I have no one nearby in Boston. When I went to make an application [for subsidized housing], the girl told me, "You need special preference, that's your case." Then I used to go and check with her, but then they put another girl over there. Those people are liars over there, that's all.

I'll Die If I Leave the North End

I separated all these papers [for her case in housing court] and I try to put them all to-gether. I sit down and I choose all the papers that belong-a to me. Any house [elderly housing] that I gotta the application, I put together. But, my god, I'm sick and tired of doing things because I'm alone and I'm old and, after all, I'm tired to do these things. See, when I read and write and do things like that, you get tired. I am an aged person [whispering]. What can I do? I can't do more than that. Sometime I think and I feel so tired. I don't have to think too much—I go to bed many times and I can't even sleep. What a-trouble I got in my life, I say to myself. Sleep? How can I? How many times I try not to think of it so it won't ruin my life, and sometimes . . . you can't help it . . . when you got trouble, you think. I don't know what's gonna be for me. What can I say—that's funny things to think of, sometimes you can't help it. The people are stupid, they don't understand the situation—they don't know and that's it. But I understand my situation and I think I'm in trouble that way. I don't know what God give me! The doctor gave me Valium and he told me if I'm really in trouble and you can't stand it no more, you can have one. But very seldom I take them—I cut them in half. But I know those are no good. I understand these things, I'm not a person to be really stupid [laughs]. I try not to stay home because when I'm home I got too much time to think. I try to do something with my hands, so when you do something *a lieto* or *contenta,* you know, make-a happy. In Italiano, *a lieto É una grande parola, voul dire "happy" in Italiano.* [You know, the word *lieto* is a great word in Italian, it means to be happy, contented.] So I try to keep my mind *alietata* [happy], you know, if I keep my mind like that, I'll be all right. Please, I don't want to leave the North End—after sixty-two years? I'll die before I leave.

Santa and Bernadine Cacciola were two sisters in their early seventies who lived together in an apartment house with eight other families. They described their daily tensions with the landlord, who eventually evicted all eight families to build condominiums.

OUR LANDLADY GETS *ARRAGIATA*

We're both afraid—if we say one word out of the way to her [the landlord], she'll kill me. She's taking care of the building for her brother-in-law as if she's the landlord. She says she's been too good to us, you know, the rents. What she meant was that we don't pay enough. She always seems to pick on us. What happened was the upstairs tenant had her door open and she was saying, "Now that's a fine thing they're doing, what your brother-in-law did to us!" [serving eviction notices] And that started it and then I put my little two cents in—I don't what I said, but it must have been something that angered her because she started yelling. She's a funny girl. When she has trouble, something goes wrong in her house, she calls me, she calls me to help her and I go down and do things for her, whatever it is. Now the other day her refrigerator broke and she came up and asked me if she could put her stuff in my freezer. So I looked in there and don't you know I took all my stuff out so she could put all kinds of meat that she had. So I said to her, "Why don't you ask the lady next door to you?" She said, "No, I'm ashamed." One time she got locked out and she stayed in my house for two hours. And she treats me like that? She's a wild one, like they say in Italian when she gets mad she's *arragiata,* you know, like crazy, wild. She wants us out in five months, how can we get out in five months? We wanted to give him a raise. He [landlord] said no, I'll make about $150,000, why should I continue with that rent?

{ *Elvira DiMattia, seventy-two, was often called to speak as a community advocate at neighborhood meetings.* }

CONDOS SHOULD BE OUT

Condominiums should be absolutely out. I know people right on my own street, nice Italian families that came to live there and now they're all looking for rooms because they have to get out. The house was sold to a new landlord. And they're nice people. And when you start getting rid of people like that, the North End changes. And that's exactly what the mayor wants! He's not making it easy for anyone to live here. And with the extraordinary expenses of the city—he's spending money like a drunken sailor. I tell them that [at community meetings] when they ask me to talk. When did you get a $20,000 raise? For me to get between three and five dollars raise, I had to work for it.

Theresa D'Alelio (left) and Josephine Zizza (right)—elderly landladies who refused to evict their poor tenants ▶

POOR TENANT,
POOR LANDLORD

▲ Tommasina Cerundolo, elderly landlady (left), Jennie Violanto, poor tenant (right), 1982

CHAPTER TWENTY

Poor Tenant, Poor Landlord

Fa cose buone É scordatelo, ma fa male É pensaci.
[Do good and forget it, but do something bad, and think of it.]

—Old proverb

— *A network of elderly women* landlords struggling with rising taxes and maintenance costs on their homes formed an undocumented safety net for their old-time elderly tenants who could not afford rising rents. Faced with the choice of selling their homes and living in subsidized housing or moving in with children outside the North End, they chose minimal raises in their rents and resisted converting their buildings into luxury condominiums. By choosing to maintain their elderly tenants in their apartments, these landlords represented the last support system of old neighborhood stability.

When I asked Josie Zizza about the difficulties of being a poor landlady in an era of rising real estate values, she spoke for the compassion and loyalty that she and other landlords like her still had for their less-fortunate neighbors.

ON BEING A POOR LANDLORD

I can't sell my house—where would I go? I wouldn't be able to get into subsidized housing—they'd say I had too much money. I give my old-time tenants heat, hot water, and six rooms for $170! I have another elderly tenant, but she's disabled. One's been here for seventeen years. And I've been here all my life. I don't drive. I have four sons [all living in the suburbs]—who wants another mother? My sister lives upstairs. How can I take care of anything when something breaks and when they see a woman—and they, well, it's not easy. Taxes go up, water bills go up. But I can't see not letting my tenants have a washing machine. Landlords are bad if they raise the rent. It would be nice if my tenants said, you've been good to us—here's $20 extra—but they don't. At least I know them—they watch the house when I'm gone, so I tell my sons I'm OK, not to worry. Where am I gonna go?

{ *Ann Ciriello was a seventy-four-year-old landlord who refused to evict her elderly tenant. She was living alone at the time of our interview.* }

My Poor Old Tenant

I have two old Italian tenants living in my apartment house for over fifty years. We just can't evict them. She [my tenant] was accepted at the Casa Maria [elderly housing], but she came to me and said, "The only way they'll take me out of my apartment will be in a box." So I said, "You'll be better off in a new building, you'll have heat." She answered me, "What are you trying to do, throw me out?" I said, "Oooh, no! I'm just trying to explain to you that I can't afford to give you more conveniences." She cried just at the thought that we didn't want her. She's been with us since I was twelve. I'm seventy-four now.

▲ Mary Cimino and her eighty-three-year-old tenant, Chiarina D'Amato

{ *During this interview, we heard someone calling from the the stairway. Helen Luongo's tenant knocked on the door and opened it slowly. In Italian she asked if Helen was all right and that she was leaving the building. As she left, Helen said, "She always does that, Anthony, just to make sure."* }

LISTEN FOR MY RADIO

My upstairs tenant is here for eighteen years. If I go out, I have peace of mind. Two years ago I asked her if I could raise her rent two dollars. She said, "Helen, you gotta take five dollars, I know you're not gettin' enough money." This is the kind of people I have—why should I go lookin' for trouble? But still, how many of them [landlords] have done what they've told me

▲ Helen Luongo and her tenant sitting on front stairs on Salem Street

to do, and I wouldn't do it—put the house in my children's name and put my name in welfare—I sacrificed my life that I don't know how many hours I've worked—and I'm still working. I made a pattern, I ironed all that material, and I cut the valance—that's what I just did. And I'm seventy-three. My kids are mad—they say, "When are you gonna give up?" I feel if I have—it isn't much—I feel if I have anything of my own—it won't pressure the children, bcause the children worry, "Ma, how ya doin?" Yes, they're good to me. One's got two boys in college. Why take it away from them when they need it?

You know who takes care of me? The woman upstairs, between the two of us, we plan it—if she's away, I'm not away. But if it happens that I'm alone—eeehh, God, who you gonna call [laughing]? Whatya gonna do? You're alone! It isn't no joke to live alone, don't you worry—it isn't a joke—especially when you're used to the family—and I have nine grandchildren, and you feel, here you are with such a big family, and you're all alone—but, uh, you just learn how to live with it. Like her [the tenant], I have her key, she has the key to my house, and we've told each other—in the morning now she knows the minute I get up—I have the transistor radio in bed with me going all night so I feel I have someone in the house. My radio or television is going all the time. My tenant is seventy [laughing], we're both old ladies—so who's gonna take care of who? And I told her, "If in the morning, you get up, and you don't hear the radio going, come in and see that for sure I'll be in bed— I'm dead! Call the undertaker, call my children!" What are you gonna do?

GOING IT ALONE

Going It Alone

Una mama campa cento figli, ma cento figli non campano una mama.
[A mother can take care of a hundred children,
but a hundred chidren can't take care of one mother.]

—Old proverb

— *In 1982, amidst much fanfare* and the support of the community, the North End Nursing Home officially opened for business. The new institution replaced the old Italian family unit, which historically relied on children to support their elders in advanced age. Now separated from their sons and daughters who lived in the suburbs of Boston, the elderly faced uncertain futures, yet refused family assistance for fear of becoming burdens to their children. Despite having cared for their parents and grandparents when they were younger while raising sons and daughters, the last of the old North Enders carried on alone.

{ *Returning to America after several years in Sicily, Frances Lauro said, "I fell in love with the North End as soon as I got here."* }

TAKING CARE OF MY GRANDMOTHER

I was born on North Street in the North End. My mother died when I was six and my father took us back to his town, Sciacca in Sicily, so my grandmother could take care of me and my brother. I hadn't even gone to school yet and my grandmother got sick and she was in bed.

I had to take care of her. I can remember standing in the doorway and she was already dead in the bed and a neighbor came by and took us home for the night. We slept on the stone floor—the rooms used to be all made of stone. The next day we went and got my grandmother

◄ A peasant woman reading her prayerbook in the village of Pisticci

and they put her on their shoulders like they did in those days, and they carried her to the casket and buried her. My brother was four years older than me, and they put him out to watch the sheep. The neighbor used to shave my hair close so I wouldn't get any bugs—maybe that's why my hair grew so thick later! Then, one of the women who was coming to America took us back to my father.

My children were all born on North Street. We were one clique—all from the same town in Italy. At that time we were stupid; now, they do this and they do that and they don't have any kids. I used to have one after another. They all grew up at once—it was nice, at least they were all one family on North Street. They used to sit in the doorways, we used to sing, kids used to play hopscotch, you know—beautiful! Now they don't believe in that no more—they got their boyfriends waiting on the corner.

FRANCES, LET ME DIE UNDER THE STOVE

I keep myself—not that I keep myself, only God keeps us up—but I went through a lot. My mother-in-law was very sick—she was confined in bed. And I had three children and one was coming. We had no washing machine in those days—I had the big tub—wash the clothes, hang 'em up, take care of her—poor soul—I was so busy I didn't know who my neighbors were. They used to say, "Why don't you put her in the home?" No! While I can do it, I'll do it. I couldn't see that. And she used to tell me, you know, the old people used to say, "Put me under the stove, don't take me away from here." She used to say, "Frances"—she used to love me—"Frances, let me die under the stove." I said to her, "Don't worry, as long as I'm living, I'll take care of you." And really and to the last minute, she was passing away, she called me, and I was right there with her. And in Italy, the same thing, honey, with my grandmother. And when I came over here, my father had gotten remarried and my stepmother had her mother and I had to take care of her too. I've been taking care of these old ladies like that. And that's my life, I took care of the old people. And still, my neighbor, Mary, she had a bad heart. I used to stay in the house with her—I didn't want to leave her alone—till her husband came home, see? We used to take little walks. "Is the weather nice?" "Yeah, Mary, comon, let's take a walk," and we used to go, easy, easy—she used to get tired, "Mary, do you want to sit down?" We'd sit on some doorstep. So we used to come home, she'd rest, I used to cook for her, and when her husband used to come home, I'd go away. And I lost her too. I don't know, this is my life. My heart is too soft with anybody—I feel bad for anybody, but I don't know if anybody feels bad for me [laughs]. My kids say, "Ma, if something happens, who's gonna take care of you?" I said, "God will." If I get sick, you suffer and I gotta suffer. I wanna go in three days—I always pray for that.

▲ Tom Bardetti in his cold-water flat, calendars in the background, 1981

At the time of our interview, Tom Bardetti was seventy and living alone in a starkly furnished, musty, cold-water flat. While we talked, I noticed the only decorations on his bare kitchen walls were four different calendars. Each one had been xed in pencil to mark off the days. When I asked him why, he told me he hung them up because his visiting nurse had suggested he do that to keep track of time. In his gravelly voice, puffing a cigarette, he said, "And the pictures on 'em [the calendars] make the place kinda homey-like, you know?"

ON LIVING ALONE

I ain't got no phone. I don't want no phone. I don't get that many calls. I don't make that many calls. I ain't got many people to call. Nobody goes shopping for me when I'm sick. Nobody goes. I go. Well, when I'm sick and I can't do it, I got some stuff here to eat for a coupla days, and then I . . . I have to do it myself. If I get sick, well, I'm taking a chance. The only people who visit me is a family from East Boston—they come once in a while— they ain't much help to me cuz they're not here, they can't help me. All the guys I grew up with, they all got married, they're all gone away—who's gone to New York, who's gone somewhere else—Framingham, Worcester. Guys got married, bought houses, and moved away. There's very few people that I know, see? Yeah . . . some of 'em died. And the new generation comes up and you don't know them. I know a few younger guys, but I can't depend on them.

Everything is for the family here. Marriage and life is to have children. You can have fun, too, but . . . mostly the whole thing is based on the family. A job, intelligence, training, school, and everything—raising kids—it's all built around the family, see? If a guy ain't got no family, what has he got? What is he gonna work on? He ain't got nothin'. I woke up too late [laughs]. I was asleep all that time—like Rip Van Winkle, he slept for twenty years and I slept for forty [laughs]. Yeah.

ON NURSING HOMES

An old friend of mine said he wanted to take care of me, but I never gave it a thought. They say, you come and live with me, give me your money, leave me your money and I'll feed ya, clean your clothes and help you and everything. I think that's better than a nursing home. If I go in a nursing home, it's no good—it'll be worse. But if I could go live with some friend, and live with a friend, and he'd see that my clothes were clean, and that I wore clean clothes, and help me to dress up, and help me in a lotta ways, yeah, I think that's better—that's better than going into a nursing home. The nursing home don't do nothing for you. My brother is in a nursing home. Now Rita the nurse is trying to find out for me where they put him. He got transferred from that nursing home and he's not there no more. Now, where is he? So now Rita is tryin' to find out where they put him cuz I sent him a letter last week and the letter came back "He's not here anymore." So where is he, see? When you ain't got nobody, they put you away and that's it. Who knows about you? Nobody! It's a tough life. I had a friend of mine and when he got too old, his daughter put him away in a nursing home. When they went to visit him, he didn't want to see them at all. His daughter could have taken care of him. He's only one guy! Instead of taking care of him, they put him away. And that broke his heart. The guy is too old to do those things to him, see? He can't take it—he's not used to that kind of life. The way they feed you is different, the way you live is different. He's too old to change all those things. He feels sorry that his own daughter put him away. So although you have kids, well, when you get old, and you get alone, like your wife dies, you got a daughter and you live with her—so they put you away! Screw you, they want to go out and live their own life—what the hell do they care about you? You're old, you ain't goin nowhere, see? The kids today, they do that all the time—cuz they don't know any better, and the ones that do, don't care.

MOM, I HOPE YOU GO BEFORE ME

How many times did my upstairs neighbors—he and his wife—have to come downstairs and help me pick up my mother because her legs weren't too good. My mother always used to say when asked how she was doing, "My legs are good, my body no good." That was my mother, all the time. She was kinda stubborn, she insisted she had to walk even when I wasn't there. One time at two in the morning she fell and there was a big bash—the whole family from downstairs came up in their pajamas to see what happened. They had to help me get my mother up. So that's how it was, living over here. Today, well, I don't know, if they heard a big bash, if anybody's gonna come and pick me up. But my mother always used to say—yes, you do good and God will always find someone to help you. And, you know, she was right. Too bad the young people don't believe too much in God. I'm not what you call a God person. I do believe in a hereafter and I do believe in a supreme being—being what it is, I don't know, but I always think there's somebody somewhere that's looking after us. And when I think of the things my mother used to tell me—sometimes she'd say before she passed away, "You know, in every family there's always one person who is going to be left alone." And I said, "Mom, I don't want to wish you any harm, but I hope that you go before me because if I go before you, you're gonna be left all alone and what are you gonna do, because with your legs . . . " She said, "It doesn't make any difference, God will take care of me if I'm all alone." And do you know, she was right because now I have all these nice people [neighbors] that when I need help, before I open my mouth, I get help. So that's why there must be somebody someplace—whether it's upstairs or what—that looks after us. It doesn't have to be a man, it doesn't have to be a certain color, but there's something somewhere. Would you call that a philosophy? Well, that's the way I look at it.

LET ME GO QUICKLY

I saw a show on television the other day about a new pneumonia injection. If I've got to get an injection not to get pneumonia and get something else, like cancer that killed a lot of younger people in my family, I'd rather have pneumonia—inside nine days, you're gone. I wonder if I'm selfish saying this, but I've seen pain, bad pain, and I hope to God nobody would get that pain—it's no good, no good. But today, then they get you better, then you get it again, then they get you better, and you get it again—that's not helping you. Like at my age now, if I get pneumonia, then they let me come back. Well, I get better, I'm not gonna feel half as good as I am now—that takes a lot out of you. So then I get it again and they're gonna do something else to me and I come back—I'm gonna feel even a little lower. Well, that's not living. They say now—we want people to live long. Yes, providing you can get around. I don't know—that's the way I feel at my age—I'll be seventy-five pretty soon, so if I get something—Oh God! I just want to go [laughs]. But look, we all have to go. Everything that's born, anything that breathes has to die, huh? Even a plant . . . has to die . . . so . . . we die [voice picks up] and as my father used to say [laughing], they used to have the funniest saying, *"Se nessuno muore qua, come ci capimmo?"* Or sometimes, *"Allo cimitero come adda riempi, con 'o capo d'ciuccio?"* That means if everyone lived and nobody ever died, how would we fill up the cemeteries—with donkey heads? [laughs] It was fun living with them.

{ *Josie Zizza spoke proudly about taking care of her mother at home until the end. Josie recognized the change that had taken place in the Italian family and lent her support for the North End Nursing Home in 1982.* }

TAKING CARE OF OUR MOTHER

We were good to my mother. She was sick for twelve years. She died at home. The doctors advised us to put her in a nursing home—we said no. She died at home and we were all there—all of us. We used to take turns taking care of her every day. I used to work four days a week, so Tuesday was my day—we all had a day each to care for my mother. We all did our share.

{ *Vladimir Ciani presided over his own men's club where many animated card games took place. He often made pizza as a treat for his friends. "Pensa a mangiare bene," [one has to think about eating well] he said at the end of our interview.* }

SOON THE NORTH END WILL BE A MEMORY

As I say, a good part of the old imprint, of this nucleus which represents so to speak a part of our Old Country transplanted in a typical American city such as Boston is fast fading and will soon disappear in its entirety. When you walk through Hull Street and North Street, Sheafe Street and Salem Street and Hanover Street—and instead of seeing Italian names on doors, you begin to notice instead the Ryans, McGraths, and Russells and so forth, and other typical American names, you can't help but put two and two together.

What's happening, one would ask. It's not so hard to figure out. The Italian landlords are remodeling at a fast pace, all the old buildings and shacks, making them very habitable and very attractive. But after these embellishments, these rents, naturally enough, jump to $200, $300, and even $400 a month! Result: The Italians as a rule are not able to pay these exorbitant rents and have to make an exit to other towns where rents still remain relatively cheap. The net result of all this is that within a decade our old North End will disappear as a symbol of our Italianity. It will only remain as a memory of what it once was. But then again, we should never lose sight of the fact that history for centuries has always repeated itself. In our case, it's happening exactly as history prescribes: Ninety years ago, we, the Italians, especially from 1890 to 1914, came to Boston in huge quantities with the net result that we displaced all the Irish and Jewish people from the North End, and we made this little corner of Boston our own. Is it any wonder that we in turn should see this process duplicated?

▼ North End overview, 1980

PHOTO CREDITS

(Cover photo) Mariangela D'Antonio (A. Riccio)
Several months after this picture was taken, Mariangela's landlord began converting the upstairs apartment to a condominium. The workers appeared at 7:00 every morning, working late into the evening and throwing debris from the window to the sidewalk below her window. The dust and soot covered her apartment, and the noise caused her much distress. One day, as she looked up to the second floor to see what the workers were up to, Mariangela lost her balance and fell, breaking her hip. Vowing to a neighbor to come back once she healed, Mariangela never returned.